Man and His Past

Man and His Past

THE NATURE AND ROLE

OF HISTORIOGRAPHY

Serge Gagnon

Translated by Margaret Heap

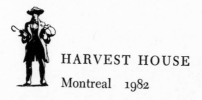

HARVEST HOUSE

Montreal   1982

Copyright © 1982 by Harvest House Ltd.

Deposited in the Bibliotheque Nationale of Quebec
3rd quarter 1982

Typography and cover: Book Design & Production
Associates, Bynum, N.C.

Printed in Canada

First Harvest House Edition

Canadian Cataloguing in Publication Data

Gagnon, Serge, 1939-
   Man and his past

Translation of: La nature et le rôle de l'historio-
graphie.
Includes index.
ISBN 0-88772-215-6

I. Historiography.   I. Title.

D13.G3313   907'.2   C82-090054-0

Contents

Acknowledgments

The author wishes to thank especially the untold numbers of Canadian taxpayers who assure the financing of universities and granting bodies. Without them, this work which was written in such time as is available for research by university teachers, would never have seen the light of day. Since I composed the lines which follow while teaching at the University of Ottawa, I am pleased to thank that institution. Thanks are due to my colleague, Hubert Watelet, of the same university, who provided me with the elements of a critical dialogue on the ins and outs of historical science. To Maynard Gertler, my thanks for his great understanding; he taught me the rudiments of the equally admirable and mysterious world of publishing.

This book has been published with the help of a grant from the Social Science Federation of Canada, using funds provided by the Social Sciences and Humanities Research Council of Canada. We also gratefully acknowledge a translation grant from the Canada Council.

Man and his Past

INTRODUCTION:

Toward a sociology
of historical knowledge

When eras are on the decline, all tendencies are subjective . . . when matters are ripening for a new
epoch, all tendencies are objective.[1]

With its characteristic emphasis on analysis of interpretations, the history of history puts itself in a somewhat
paradoxical situation. How can it be taken seriously when it
begins with the assumption that all knowledge is subjective?
Logically, the historiographer who undertakes to reflect on
the knowledge of others from a sociological perspective must
recognize that his own work is itself conditioned by various
psychological and social factors.

The purpose of this essay is to present the relativist thesis
on historical knowledge, illustrating it with examples drawn
from French-Canadian historiography. Our aim is to "domes-
ticate" and popularize a school of thought with which historians here are not necessarily acquainted. We have not
attempted an exhaustive survey of the literature in the field.
The reader may wonder why some excellent, and indeed
classic, works are not mentioned; the answer is that a more
detailed survey was impossible in the framework of a short
essay.

1

Some terms should be clarified at the outset. Terms like relativism or subjectivism are, in our opinion, a more or less explicit confession that the historian consciously or unconsciously adopts the biases of his era, national milieu, social "class," generation, etc. The objectivist historians, by contrast, emphasize increasingly refined methods along with the cumulative—and indeed relatively definitive—nature of knowledge. Generally speaking, the latter reject as futile the idea of trying to establish a relationship between knowledge, on the one hand, and the individual or society that apprehends that knowledge, on the other. They do not think this is worth examining. They prefer to consider history purely as knowledge, and generally take little interest in knowledge as a cultural expression. Consequently, the history of historical writing is only a legitimate endeavor for them inasmuch as it deals with the history of progress in historical methods. It goes without saying that there are many different shades of opinion in both schools of historians. At one end of the spectrum, there is the openly and publicly committed historian; and at the other, the historian who claims to stand outside of time and geography.

The history of historiography is a fairly new field of historical study. Not so very long ago, one of its practitioners pointed out that its object was not yet very clearly defined in Great Britain.[2] In the Soviet Union, the convenient division of the globe into capitalist and socialist countries, and more especially the equally convenient division of history into the eras of slavery, feudalism, capitalism and ultimately the dictatorship of the proletariat, undoubtedly help explain why the problem of the history of history has already been settled there. The evolution of the historical approach is determined by the dialectics of class struggle. But this approach is encumbered by the need to vindicate and justify, and historians in the liberal democracies do not find it flexible enough to satisfy them.[3] Our remarks apply equally well to the Marxist theory of historical knowledge, at least in its most orthodox version. In *History and Truth*, Adam Schaff rejects Mannheim's theses on the subjective nature of all knowledge and argues, for example, that a historian's objectivity is dependent on his adherence to the cause of the proletariat. By doing so, the historian achieves part of (not partial) truth, aligning himself with historical progress toward classless society, which is the absolute truth.[4] In our opinion, this approach is no more valid than the former providential determinism. The Marxist approach is just as subjective as the approaches rooted in other ideological tendencies.

＊　　＊　　＊

I begin with a brief survey of how some of the major schools of historical thought have reacted to the relativist thesis. As we will see in the following pages, it has been embraced most enthusiastically by the British and American schools of history. It is no coincidence that these are also the circles in which the study of historiography is most flourishing. Subsequently, I will further examine the nature and role of historical research, using a literature that is not usually dealt with by historians: psychology, sociology, philosophy and even theology all have something to offer the historian in his reflection on the nature of his work. Together, I hope, this will provide a preliminary theoretical framework for the history of historiography, a vast field of intellectual history—socio-cultural history, as the Europeans call it.[5]

I. The relativist thesis and contemporary Western schools of history

In his article, "La fonction sociale de l'histoire,"[1] Fernand Dumont voices the hope that the "history of history become a very major part of research and training in our universities." So far, the study of how successive generations of historians have depicted our past has not interested our historians sufficiently. More often than not, historical thought here has been treated to an all-too-superficial evaluation in literary histories and critical works more concerned with singling out its stylistic qualities and flaws than with seriously analyzing its contents as such.[2] Professional historians have not had much to say about it either, apart from a few articles and even fewer books. There are, nonetheless, several exceptions: Pierre Savard has provided a good outline of the place and development of historical writing in our literary heritage. But he focused too much on the progress in knowledge and the organization of the discipline, and neglected to relate the ideological contents of historical production to society itself.[3] His lack of interest in a sociology of historical writing is perhaps in part a reflection of our faithfulness to French intellectual traditions.

French historians have never greeted the history of historiography with much enthusiasm. Guy Palmade remarked on this indifference in an essay he wrote on the subject.[4]

Jean Glénisson also mentions the "indifference of almost the entire French school of historians to the history of history."[5] Like Marrou, he sees it as a consequence of the French school's profound distrust for the philosophy of history. Raymond Aron came to a similar conclusion in his *Introduction to the Philosophy of History*.[6]

Despite this indifference, occasionally bordering on contempt, some thinkers have nevertheless recognized the relative nature of historical knowledge. In 1949, Lucien Febvre wrote: ". . . history inevitably gathers, classifies and groups together facts about the past in terms of its current needs. It interrogates the dead in terms of the living."[7] As an example, he points to historians' use of the personal archives of the French nobility. Although these papers became available to historians a few decades after the French revolution, it was almost a century before they were recognized and used as important sources for economic history—an indication that historians' questions have their roots in more or less contemporary concerns. More recently, Philippe Wolff has echoed the words of Febvre: "The current enthusiasm for 'economic and social history' is actually a phenomenon of our civilization. Since the middle of the 19th century, there has been an acceleration of economic development which has highlighted social problems. That is why historians have tended to take an interest in this aspect of society's past."[8]

This line of thinking led Febvre to propose a sociology of historical knowledge: "The social function of history can be described as the organization of the past in terms of the present. This aspect of our work has not been studied by anyone either. People have worked on the theory of history; no one has worked on the sociology of history."[9] He reaffirmed the relativity of history in a well-known dictum: "History also creates its own subject. It does not create it once and for all.

In other words, all history is a product of its era. Indeed, there is no History, but only historians."[10]

Alphonse Dupront, one of the pioneering figures in the study of the history of mentalities, attaches great importance to the history of historiography:

The history of historiography is practically a virgin field . . . contemporary historians have too often forgotten that history is by its very nature a relative science. . . . History has become our history, the history we write and read in our era, the history that expresses our capacity to analyze the past in us and establish lines of communication between this living past and the other, allegedly dead past that nonetheless continues to mark the present. . . . In other words, a kind of exchange with the past is established . . . era by era. . . . The historian has a method . . . and makes choices in the history he writes. These choices may be the active, conscious choices of the historian himself, or they may be passive choices, inherited from his social environment. They may lie somewhere between the two, a means of being heard by that environment. And in these choices, one sees a succession of images or data from the traditional, collective memory. . . .[11]

But apart from such declarations of principle, it must be admitted that French historians generally do not like to ponder the social significance of their work. In practice, French historiography has more or less resisted the relativist thesis. It is only interested in the history of historical writing inasmuch as it illustrates—as is the case with the history of other sciences—the progress made in terms of methodology and historical knowledge.[12] However, a history of historical writing turned toward the social and cultural future of a group or community cannot be restricted to a study of the origins of historical methodology. This is certainly a legitimate subject for study in the methodological context, but it is not a statement of the nature of historical interrogation. As Fernand Dumont has written: "Each new situation implies a reinterpretation of the past. It is not simply a matter of gradually improving our documentation or analytical techniques . . . the past is not a sum of unchanging memories . . . our relationship to the past is in a constant state of change. The problems and crises of today raise new and original questions about the past, which is a living memory in which our heritage meets up with today's commitments. The science of history must reiterate this for each new generation."[13]

Seen in this light, the current fashion for social history is, like economic history, a phenomenon of our times. The recently evolved notion of participatory democracy and the upsurge of interest in the socialist tradition are not unrelated to the new place of the masses in historical writing. Since Marx, in particular, the study of the laboring classes has gradually come to challenge the reign of great men and outstanding personalities in historiography. Economic and social history have gained ground at the expense of political and diplomatic history.

All this has naturally enriched our perception of past societies. But it cannot be denied that the new approaches to history are in part motivated by ideological considerations. As Walsh put it: "It is at any rate partly because our estimation of the common man has changed, because ordinary people are no longer regarded as they were in a more aristocratic age, that the common people have come to figure so largely in our histories."[14] The French school of history tends, however, to gloss over the social and ideological implications of this obvious trend. For instance, the methodologist Paul Veyne has just written a violent diatribe against the school of historical relativism. He considers that only the nationalist historians of the 19th century and their descendents may be rightly characterized as having an ideological bias in their historical outlook.[15] So it is not surprising that *The Meaning of History*, published in 1954 by the historian and philosopher Henri Marrou, was not greeted with much enthusiasm by French historians. Nor did Raymond Aron's thesis, a fine critical philosophy of history, shake their faith in their established priorities: the primary concern of historians is to perfect their tools and methods, not to indulge in philosophical speculations. This has led Jean Glénisson to conclude that French historians today reflect something of the ambitions of the positivist school at the turn of the century. For although the *Annales* school of historians derides the positivists (whose approach to history is described, with more than a touch of irony, as historicist and factual), both schools are characterized by the same resolutely scientific intention. They are both confident of their capacity to know the past better and more fully than have former generations, and they share the same concern with putting epistemology at the center of the historian's work of reflection.[16] Ignoring the social dimension of historiography, they implicitly endow historical work with a certain objectivity, as if it were divorced from any specific time or era. This attitude is well illustrated in a recent review of French historiography by Michel François.[17] François emphasizes the organization of research and the achievements of the French school of history to such an extent that the figure of the historian pales beside the impressive portrait of how knowledge has progressed. In *The Historian's Craft*, Marc Bloch suggested that the present be used to understand the past. François comments, "I myself would add, yes, but on condition that the present not be projected into the past, which is the worst way to write history."[18] Other contributors are not so prudent: they discuss at length the status of the historian in German, British, and American society and his present-minded vision of the past.

The contemporary historian in Anglo-German circles has

remained more relativist than his French colleagues. In West Germany, professional historians are perplexed and sceptical about the achievements of the *Annales* school. They are not particularly sympathetic to the kind of social and economic history practiced by their neighbors, with their concept of the "longue durée," their quantitative approach, their study of the "common man," and their historical demography. German historians still have a marked preference for intellectual and political history more or less equated with State history.[19]

Although British historians in their work adhere to the "scientific intention" of the French school in many respects,[20] they have also retained an interest in the subjectivity of the historian. True, John B. Bury wrote in 1903 (the year of Simiand's "manifesto") that history was a "science, no more and no less,"[21] but Carr has pointed out that in the following fifty years this dictum was rarely quoted. When British historians did so, Carr suggests, it was usually to deride Bury's allegedly naive confidence.[22] Thus it is hardly surprising that the relativist theses of the Italian historian and philosopher Benedetto Croce have met with a sympathetic hearing in Britain, while in France his major works have only recently been translated.[23] In the 1920s and 1930s, R. G. Collingwood, another historian and philosopher, became the British Croce.[24]

Collingwood's *The Idea of History*, first published in 1946, is one of the most relativist extant theses on historical knowledge. Collingwood placed particular emphasis on what he called the historical imagination.[25] His exploration of the imaginary led him to compare and in many ways equate works of history with literature[26] and painting.[27] This comparison was subsequently repeated by Walsh, Marrou (at least as far as biographies were concerned), Halkin and, indirectly, Samuel Eliot Morrison, who said, "The historian can learn much from the novelist."[28] They dealt in fact, however, with two kinds of comparisons. For Collingwood, it meant that the historian, like the novelist or painter, draws on his imagination to structure what he has to say and fills in the blanks with what may well be fragmentary documentation. For others—and especially for the biographer—the comparison also means that the study of history provides the historian with a view of human destinies that are just as captivating as the characters in a novel. Thus, for instance, Narcisse-Eutrope Dionne, one of our 19th-century historians, wrote that the life of Father Jogues was "a veritable novel"; and Joseph-Edmond Roy also described Lahontan's history as "a veritable novel." Benjamin Sulte, another 19th-century French-Canadian historian, was much more explicit, confessing: "I have read novels. But not one of them measures up to the study of history, the longest novel. D'Iberville's campaigns are just as exciting and just as fascinating as Dumas's *Three Musketeers*."[29] Enough has been said. The mutual influence of history and the historical novel in the romantic school is common knowledge.[30]

Collingwood's thought, like that of Croce, owes much to idealist philosophy. For both these historians, the past as a subject of knowledge does not exist. The job of the historical imagination is to imagine the past, "not an object of possible perception, since it does not now exist, but able through this activity to become an object of our thought."[31] This evokes Croce's dominant theme in *History as the Story of Liberty*, and explains why Collingwood, basing himself on Croce, wrote, "Instead of answering the question how the past is known we should be maintaining that the past is not known, but only the present." This is certainly the thesis of the Italian historian. All history is contemporary. The historian rethinks the past and brings it into the present once again.[32] This is still the thesis defended in Britain by some historians who accept the relativist point of view. Certainly, as Walsh has pointed out, "it seems absurd to maintain . . . that his [the historian's] whole reconstruction is radically false."[33] Nonetheless, the historian cannot ignore the whole series of factors that condition the very act of knowing. The historian, his milieu, his personality, his era, are all factors that influence his perceptions in the light of the fears, aspirations, anxieties or certitudes of his contemporaries. Herbert Butterfield's historiography is partially based on this assumption.[34] The interviews published by Peter Geyl in 1955 were an indication of a certain "tolerance" on the part of British historians today, inasmuch as many of them now recognize the relativist thesis and indeed themselves submit to the test of subjectivity.[35]

However, the "promised land" of the subjectivist position is really to be found in the United States. Generally speaking, American historical circles willingly admit the subjective nature of historical knowledge. This comes across clearly in *The Historian's Workshop,* a collection of autobiographical accounts.[36] For our neighbors, history is still the mistress of life, as the historians of a former generation were so fond of repeating. Richard Hofstadter sees this pragmatic approach as a reflection of American society itself. "In the American temperament, there is a powerful bias toward accepting the pragmatic demand upon history: it is hard for us to believe that there is such a thing as a truth that cannot be made useful," he writes in the conclusion to his study of the progressive historians.[37] Hofstadter points out that the difference between George Bancroft, who helped forge a national American consciousness, and Charles A. Beard, who wrote during the interwar years under the influence of the Welfare State and the Depression, is related more to their eras than to the fundamental attitudes of American historians toward the study of the past.[38]

Charles Beard, the leading "committed" historian of the 1930s, can be called the Collingwood or Croce of the United States. His favorable review of Collingwood's work in 1947 is certainly no coincidence.[39] He had previously invited Croce to comment on his 1934 manifesto, "Written History as an Act of Faith"—thus clearly illustrating how close his thinking was to that of the European relativists.[40] Rankean objectivism was the main target of Beard's vehement attack in his plea for pragmatic history. Ranke was hardly an objective historian, Beard argued; on the contrary, he was a conservative.

The formula itself ["*Wie es eigentlich gewesen*"] was a passing phase of thought about the past. Its author, Ranke, a German conservative, writing after the storm and stress of the French Revolution, was weary of history written for, or permeated by, the purpose of revolutionary propaganda. He wanted peace. The ruling classes of Germany, with which he was affiliated, having secured a breathing spell in the settlement of 1815 wanted peace to consolidate their position. Written history that was cold, factual, and apparently undisturbed by the passing of time served best the cause of those who did not want to be disturbed.[41]

Basically, Beard held that objectivity is a myth, cultivated by the 19th century, with its concern for preserving social peace and heading off all change. In short, as Skotheim has written, Beard's act of faith "was that history was moving progressively toward a collectivist democracy. Thus, to Beard, the historian's function was to create a progressive future . . . the historian was a scholar who used his knowledge of the past to improve the present."[42]

Progressive historians like Beard and Vernon Parrington believed that the historian unavoidably expressed his affiliations. Ultimately, they saw the cold, factual account as a prudent façade for an interpretation of events that served the ruling classes. It is noteworthy that American sociology has developed along somewhat the same lines as those reflected in American historical circles. C. Wright Mills, author of the manifesto, *The Sociological Imagination*,[43] defended a position vis-à-vis "value-free sociology" that was similar to the theses of the progressive historians. Mills held that intellectuals, as free and enlightened men, had the obligation to assume the moral leadership of public life. He went so far as to accuse his colleagues of being responsible for the conservative nature of American society and of being accomplices of the ruling classes. His last work, published in the year of his death, treats Marxism as a valid methodology.[44] Mills thus pioneered a new orientation in the social sciences in the United States. Beginning with the basic assumption that American society is ill, the "New Left Sociology, Economics and Political Science"[45] formulate value judgments in their empirical research, diagnose and prescribe solutions. A growing number of their specialists insist on using what they consider to be a better society as a reference point for any study of the mechanisms and functioning of today's society. In a parallel development, the "consensus" of the 1940-60 period[46] was followed by the emergence of a "New Left" in American historical thinking.[47] Like Beard and his contemporaries, these neo-progressives are committed to playing an active role in the movements of protest that have characterized American society since the Kennedy era. This is what Staughton Lynd, one of these new historians, has to say: "I believe Marxism is correct in its understanding of where humanity has been and is going. . . . The historian who does not grasp the fact that mankind, whatever else it is doing, is making an agonized transition from societies that are based on private property to societies that are not, is in my view out of touch with what is happening in the second half of the twentieth century."[48]

It would be an exaggeration to present the American historical analysis exclusively as the result of more or less consciously and voluntarily subjective approaches. In the United States, as in France and Great Britain, historians are concerned with the scientific purpose and direction of their work. Quantitative history and the history of the "common man" are two major aspects of American historical research.[49] But generally speaking, the history written by our American neighbors is closer to the relativist historical tradition than it is to the work of French historians. Nor does one find in the United States the gap that exists in France between the professional historian and those who reflect critically on the nature and role of history. This alone is enough to explain why the history of history is such a flourishing field of study in the United States. As a matter of fact, the best historiographical essays have probably been produced by American historians. John Higham's essay points the way to an authentic sociology of historical knowledge—through the study of the status of the historian and his place in the social structure, the study of the professionalization of the historian's craft, and an understanding of the consumers of the historical product.[50]

II.   Historian and document: the personal memoir

Documents are the historian's raw materials. Since until recently historians have given precedence to qualitative accounts, it is worth taking some time to consider their value.

To be really complete, a discussion of the relative nature of history would have to consider the sources destroyed by the historical actors themselves, by those who conserved the archives, by the immediate "descendants," or by those who continued their work. Similarly, some collections and some archives are, for various reasons, inaccessible. In admitting that the available sources do not contain the entire past, we recognize the innate selectivity present in historical writing even before the historian begins his research. But over-emphasizing this only leads to pointless scepticism. Suffice it to say that the historian works with the available sources. The question then becomes whether these documents can enable him to discover history as it really happened.

At the time when Ranke, Seignobos, John Adams, or John Bury worked, the level of refinement of historical criticism hardly allowed them or anyone else to question the value of personal or firsthand accounts; the test of credibility settled all doubts. Marx and Freud, however, and more generally all the discoveries made in psychology, have undermined many former certitudes. Each witness records and stores a memory of the events he observes or lives through. But time, his social position, and age, all influence what he selects to remember; and memories are always reconstructed in keeping with social, ethnic, and generational biases. The result is that the value of the memoir is relative, regardless of how rigorously it is criticized.[1] The account is therefore an extremely fragile instrument of knowledge. "The criticism of personal memoirs," Piéron has written, "has shown us that *memory* is fundamentally unfaithful, considering what it *leaves out* and what it *distorts*."[2]

Generally speaking, discoveries about the psychology of personal memoirs have simply caused historians to reiterate the value of historical criticism. While psychologists saw in personal documents a revelation of the mental life of their authors (think, for example, of the travelers' accounts so often cited by historians), historians did not see why this discovery should in any way invalidate the traditional critical method.[3] A passage by Louis Gottschalk is indicative of this attitude:

To . . . [the] psychologist it is the degree of subjectivity in these documents that distinguishes them from other documents. Documents written in the first person—like autobiographies and letters—or documents written in the third person but describing human reactions and attitudes—like newspaper accounts, court records, and records of social agencies—seem to be the best examples.
To the historian the difference between first-person and third-person documents is not of major significance.

He goes on to explain that an account from a direct witness is more credible than one from an indirect witness.[4] In short, the historian's work is analogous to that of a court of justice. The problem with the comparison is that the facts analyzed by historians are much more complex than those considered by judges and litigants.

In France, the psychology of human testimony and rumor

has given rise to similar reactions. In his review of the critical method in *The Historian's Craft,* Marc Bloch weighed the importance of the psychology of personal accounts. But he contented himself with illustrations which gave the lie to false witnesses. He concluded that the agreement of evidence was a valid test.[5]

If we accept Bloch's solution, it is obvious that an accumulation of concurring accounts lends added weight to the knowledge transmitted by them. This is why, for instance, Jean Hamelin concluded in his *Economie et société en Nouvelle-France* that the merchant class in the colony was not wealthy; since he did not have inventories of the merchants' possessions providing him with precise information about their fortunes, he had to make do with the concurring accounts of the intendants.[6] At best, then, the historian can achieve a moral certitude about the facts by relying on a series of personal recollections. This, after all, is the method used in legal proceedings.

Marxist history, which is more critical, remains dissatisfied with this approach. It does not consider that the judgments expressed by a group or social class are always conclusive in establishing the "truth." In the words of Pierre Vilar:

Was Marx not the first to demand of men: when you think something, first ask yourselves why you think it. And when you hear something said, first ask yourselves who said it and why—a remarkable extension of the historian's classic "internal criticism," which traditional practice too often reduces to a naive test of sincerity, skill, dissembling or elementary and base interests. The Marxist critique of evidence . . . is a sociological critique of knowledge: it does not see attitudes and thoughts as irreducible absolutes to be attributed solely to the individual. It seeks to explain these attitudes and thoughts, not with simplistic references to material interests (as is sometimes thought) but by seeing their foundations *in social space* and *in historical time.* These social and historical dimensions cannot be safely ignored in any literary or philosophical analysis.

This Marxist critique of texts, and this search for *serial documents* with a common meaning for a class or an era, is altogether another exercise with different implications than the simple "internal criticism" of personal accounts. It is the very foundation of historical science, whose essential postulates must include Marx's phrase: *we cannot judge an era from its own opinion of itself.* And we cannot judge ourselves from the opinion we *think* we have.[7]

What Vilar suggests here is that the historian should adopt an attitude of systematic doubt toward his evidence. He must not trust the witness, for the latter's version of the "facts" depends on his position in the social hierarchy. He does agree that serial records (and serial history) are more valid than individual accounts.[8] But even such documents are at most an expression of the greater or lesser subjectivity of social groups. Consequently, the historian who does not go beyond these documents generally cannot surmount the subjectivity of the age studied and cannot grasp the objective social reality. In discussing the French Revolution, Vilar winds up relativizing the value of serial documents and at the same time illustrating the scientific value of the Marxist interpretation of history: "For Michelet, Turgot's edict on the freedom of grain was the "Marseillaise of wheat," proof of what a great and generous man he was. . . . The people, who revolt, do not understand. They are wrong, they are ignorant. At times they are cruel. . . . And the poor village priests who side with the people are fanatical or narrow-minded. Or else they have bad intentions. And the aristocracy is plotting."[9]

In Vilar's mind, Michelet did not understand anything. He did not understand "that the problem was *hunger.*" Should we side with the people? With the bourgeois reformers? With neither, answers Vilar. The historian's task is simply to recognize "the reason for the people's revolt"; that is "real *objec-tivity.*" He goes on to define the approach of Marxist history: "The objective analysis of price movements and "record prof-its," of fundamental class contradictions and temporary con-tradictions between categories may seem to be "vulgar ma-terialism" for those who are irritated by our abundance of figures and studies of accounts. But it is only on the basis of such analyses that we can hope to get beyond both the sub-jectivity of the period under study and our own subjectivity."[10]

Of course, this excessive purism is not entirely convincing. As Walsh has pointed out, it is somewhat illogical to argue that all thought is subjective: "Marxists and Freudians, in their different ways, have taught us all to look for non-rational causes for ideas and beliefs which on the surface look perfectly rational, and have convinced some of us that rational thinking as such is an impossibility. But though we cannot (and should not) return to the naive confidence of our grandfathers in these matters, it must none the less be pointed out that . . . it asks us to believe, as a matter of rational conviction, that rational conviction is impossible. And this we cannot do."[11]

Given this reservation, however, it remains true that both the Marxist critique and scientific psychology force us to admit that in many instances the historian only knows the past through the more or less subjective knowledge of his wit-nesses. Furthermore, he always tends to identify with one or another of them and to reject the position of witnesses op-posed to those whose views he shares. Although he may theoretically be able to overcome his own subjectivity in studying the sources, he can rarely overcome the subjectivity of the period under study. "The history we read," said a British author, "though based on facts, is, strictly speaking, not factual at all, but a series of accepted judgments."[12] Carr applied this to medieval history and commented that the image of a devoted and religious Middle Ages comes from witnesses who moved in church circles. If this is so, he asked, how can we conclude that their accounts reflect reality? It is true that medievalists today have rounded out this rather naive version of the Middle Ages. Nothing guarantees, however, that their interpretation does not stem largely from the values of today's secular society. There is an analogy here with what Jean Blain has just written about the traditional historiography of New France. He quite rightly pointed out:

By French-Canadian historians' near-absolute dependence on a kind of source that tends to reveal much more about an ideal of colonization than about colonial reality . . . our historians have been insidiously led to write the history of the New France that *should* have been in the view of those who directed it, rather than the New France that actually was. . . . They have paid more attention to the metropolitan plan and programs of colonization. They have grasped and described colonial institutions on the basis of royal charters and edicts, treating the changes they underwent in the colony for the most part as so many deviations or exceptions. . . . They have embraced the image of colonial society projected by local and metropolitan authorities.[13]

Carr's remarks on a certain vision of the Middle Ages can be similarly applied to this kind of historiography of New France. The sociologist of historical knowledge must keep in mind that in the past our historians identified with a kind of source corresponding to a theological understanding of how history unfolds, perfectly consistent with traditional French-Canadian society. In contrast, the disintegration of the traditional social framework in turn stimulated—as Blain illustrated with his comments on the new orientations in research—a reinterpretation of the past more in keeping with the new values and new goals of Quebec society. The revisionist tendencies are due at least partly to changes in Quebec society itself, regardless of the methodological progress made and the consequent improvements in our knowledge of society under the *ancien regime*.

Distinctions have to be made, of course, between personal accounts that do not imply any value judgments and those that, on the contrary, are inseparable from a moral or subjective evaluation of reality. The history of the climate, for example, does not pose the same problems for internal criticism that the history of a revolution does. The left and the right do not enter into the study of climates. The same is true in determining the itinerary of a traveler. The positivist historians excelled at this kind of work. But the analysis of what a traveler's account says is an entirely different matter. Any evaluation of the significance of social change necessarily implies a value judgment, a specific point of view, a bias on the part of the observer. Since historians are concerned with more than chronologies and place names, they will inevitably have to use personal accounts that are subjective in varying degrees. In trying to get around the problem posed by the psychology of personal accounts, Bloch ignored the vast number of documents in which straightforward facts are mixed with value judgments. In his examples, he was careful not to criticize a source that expressed the inevitable subjectivity of its times. Halphen did the same in his *Introduction à l'histoire*.[14] His illustrations of the critical method were almost all drawn from factual history. Yet the daily practice of history shows that it is not always so easy to separate what is true from what is false. If the treatises on critical history gloss over these problems, it is certainly not because the authors do not think they are real problems; it is rather that the books are written for beginners and concerned chiefly with setting out the rules of historical method. For this reason, they use examples that can be criticized with apparent effectiveness.

III. The historian and the choice of witnesses

Thus far, we have emphasized that historiography is primarily concerned with knowing its subject as accurately as possible. But this is not how history is written in practice. More often than not, historians have paid little attention to serial documents. When they have tried to use them, the series have been too heterogeneous and too discontinuous to reveal the conscience of an age or of certain social groups. Thus, for example, some historians of French Canada have proven there was an agricultural bias in the 19th century, while others have demonstrated that there was not.[1] This can only mean that the initial selection of sources more or less reflected the authors' inclinations. At the very least, it would seem that both sides generally retained the memoirs that corresponded to preconceived ideas. In addition, they either consciously or unconsciously left out the awkward witnesses whose observations contradicted the historians' versions of reality. One of the historiographer's tasks is precisely to ascertain as best he can the ideological basis for the selection of sources. His task is not limited to examining the explicit value judgments of historians who wrote some time ago. The kind of historical writing so common in the 19th century has gradually given way to more discreet forms of subjectivity, involving choices that we will come back to later.

It would obviously be tactless, indiscreet, or foolhardy to use recent historical writings to illustrate what we call the

ideological process of selecting sources. So for the purposes of
our argument we will refer solely to the traditional body of
French-Canadian historiography.

At the end of the 19th century, Narcisse-Eutrope Dionne
published a biography of the Abbé Charles-François Painchaud, the founder of the College de Saint-Anne-de-la Poca-
tière.[2] One of our students catalogued the correspondence
Dionne copied by hand in the process of preparing the book.
The letters included a very long one written to Louis-Joseph
Papineau in which Painchaud requested a donation of 1000
pounds for the college and professed his sympathies with the
Patriotes' ideas.[3] Yet there is no mention of this letter in the
biography apart from one innocuous reference. This omission
suggests—and the rest of the book confirms—that ultramontane
historiography did not want to recognize the state's role in the
establishment of classical colleges. In any case, the relations
between Painchaud and the Patriote leader would clearly
have seemed curious in the light of the 1830s, when Papineau
and his party were in open conflict with the clergy. The fact
that someone as important as Papineau in the history of
French Canada was ignored in the biography is puzzling
unless one takes into account the author's ultramontane convictions.

The historiography of New France provides another example. Historians have quoted abundantly from Peter Kalm, one
of the travelers who visited the colony of New France. Baron
de Lahontan, however, has generally been considered an unreliable observer. In our opinion, he was ignored by French-
Canadian historians largely because of his "revolutionary"
views; for elsewhere, in Europe, his work was considered to
be of major importance—there were twenty-five unabridged
editions of his *New Voyages* . . . published between 1703
and 1758.[4] What lies behind these contrasting appreciations?

In the French tradition, Christianity was no longer the center of the universe for the thinkers of the Age of Enlightenment. Religious customs and moral standards in America and
the East were the object of "scientific" curiosity. They were
not judged in relation to Christianity as the true religion. On
the contrary, the rationalists saw in them sources of man's alien-
ation. Consequently, Amerindian customs were studied either
from an ethnological perspective or as a source of inspiration for
a new society to be built. In this sense, Lahontan was a fore-
runner of the Enlightenment. That is why 18th-century intellectuals in Europe attached so much importance to his travel
narratives. They found in them the noble savage as opposed
to the bigoted clergy and, more broadly, a social and political
regime considered decadent in comparison with primitive
civilization. In contrast, French-Canadian historians later re-
lied on missionaries' accounts each time they described Indian
customs. Lahontan's reputation as an unreliable observer is
generally associated with the "legend" of the *filles de joie*. But
historians have not forgiven him either for having observed
the indigenous population without reference to the standards
of European civilization. Joseph-Edmond Roy made this re-
proach: "Lahontan's great fault . . . was that he attributed
refined ideas and subtle feelings to the savages and expressed
opinions that did not correspond to the established order of
things among civilized nations. . . . He saw only the injustices
he suffered; embittered, he included societies and their civil
and religious institutions in the same blanket condemnation."[5]

Lahontan's popularity abroad, so unwarranted in the minds
of French-Canadian historians (most of whom were ultramontane), explains partly why Narcisse-Eutrope Dionne
wrote a book about him two hundred years after the first
edition of *New Voyages* . . . was published. He was surprised

at how well Lahontan's book had sold. He wrote in 1905: "Lahontan wrote only one book about his travels in North America, and an ill-advised one at that. So it is hard to explain why it has been popular enough to have been republished repeatedly. . . . Just recently, two new editions have been published, one in French and one in English."[6]

At the turn of the century, only a handful of anticlericalists took Lahontan seriously. The group around the *Canada-Revue* concluded:

Michelet refers to Lahontan as a trustworthy witness on what he saw in Canada between 1683 and 1692. On returning to Europe, Lahontan published . . . the fruits of his observations. . . . His comments could have been written yesterday: "The priests' persecution extends even to domestic matters and home life. They always have a watchful eye on the behaviour of women and girls. . . . To be in their good books, you have to take communion every month. . . . The priests are against books: only books of devotions are considered respectable; all others are forbidden and condemned to be burned."[7]

With the exception of this minority that applauded him, Fernch Canada has not been kind to Lahontan. He was a sorry figure in the eyes of late 19th-century historians. Roy considered that Lahontan had come to Canada devoid of any colonizing spirit. His only ambition was to recoup the lost family fortunes.[8] Unsuccessful in his attempts to "restore any semblance of the family's former splendor,"[9] Lahontan became resentful and vindictive. He turned to "bad books,"[10] sometimes in the company of unfrocked priests and apostates—judged equally objectionable.[11] His critic did recognize that he had the merit of being "innovative":[12] he was a precursor of Rousseau and Chateaubriand.[13] But all in all, he was a damned anarchist. For his Canadian biographer, "trying to change the established order of things is the eternal dream of all those who have missed their calling in life."[14] Since innovators were by definition "failures" for Roy, it is not difficult to see why he disliked Lahontan. After listing Lahontan's "vices" ("sulky and acrimonious," p. 60; "embittered, irreverent, a drinker and quarreler," p. 164; "his distorted mind, mean and naturally slanderous"), Roy condemned him unremittingly for his calumnies about the women of New France. The charge goes on for more than thirty pages;[15] the accused is found guilty (p. 189) of having been a bad soldier, having written a bad book and, above all, having dabbled in philosophy.[16]

The foregoing is a good illustration of how the selection of sources is often guided by an historian's ideological convictions. The accounts left by the Fathers Leclercq, Le Tac and Hennepin are other examples of sources rejected in part for ideological reasons.[17] Suffice it to say that if our historians have cast doubt on Lahontan's observations, it is partly because our society long refused to accept the heritage of the 18th century.

That is why we say the historian is, so to speak, a witness to his own era.[18] For example, it would be just as easy to demonstrate that our historiography of the French Regime, up to, and including Guy Frégault's *La civilisation de la Nouvelle-France*,[19] was at least in part a systematic refutation of the work of Francis Parkman, the American historian of New France. To put it another way, the historian is inevitably molded by his religious, political, social, and national beliefs and background. Let us, then, turn our attention away from the historian and his sources and direct it toward the historian's relationship to his environment.

IV. The historian and society

Carr has insisted at length on the social nature of historical knowledge. Certainly, any historian has his own psychological makeup, his own preferences. Carr's advice to those willing to listen is therefore to study the historian before beginning to study the facts. But he also sees the historian as a product of his times: "The historian, before he begins to write history, is the product of history."[1] His initial advice thus becomes: "Before you study the historian, study his historical and social environment. The historian, being an individual, is also a product of history and of society."[2] According to Carr, the influence of social factors is more decisive than what goes on in the mind of the historian. He puts this very explicitly when he says: "When you take up a historical work, it is not enough to look for the author's name on the title page: look also for the date of publication or writing—it is sometimes even more revealing."[3] Without distinguishing the psychological from the social aspects, Marrou wrote in a similar vein: "However personal a work may be, it is a response to a question confronting the social group to which the historian belongs."[4] This is why any sociology of historiography must assume right from the start that a historical work is a collective work. It constitutes the testimony of an individual socially determined by his environment, just as fiction does for the sociologist of literature. Hence, for instance, the importance of the idea of generations in analyzing historiography.[5]

27

All this, however, is only one aspect of the problem. The sociology of literature, from which our approach is provisionally borrowed,[6] is concerned with more than literary production. It is also interested in the audience for which it is produced. Just as the historian's background and leanings condition his knowledge of the past, so what he writes must reflect some of his public's expectations. Paul Ricoeur has written: "The historian's history is a *written* or professed work which, like every such work, only finds its completion in the reader, the student, and the public."[7] Thus an awareness of the historian's environment is necessary for the sociologist of historical knowledge on two counts: the historian is the product of his environment, and at the same time it is his environment that consumes what he writes. We will come back to this point later. For the time being, it is sufficient to observe that we must first understand the society to which a historian belongs before we can analyze historiography defined as a cultural expression. Conversely, the audience for the historian's work must be able to see itself in one way or another in what the historian writes.

The parallel between the author/producer and the public/consumer serves to warn the historiographer against judging the impact of historical production in the light of his sympathies for this or that interpretation. If he does not avoid the temptation of judging one work to be *truer* than another, he runs the risk of falling into the worst anachronisms, especially if he is studying the product of a former era. He may cross the line separating the sociology of knowledge from epistemology. This is where a fundamental distinction between literary works and historical works comes in.

V. Historiography as knowledge of the past

The sociology of literature dissects an era, its imagery, its sensitivity, and its values as revealed in its literature: it does not have to worry about the truth of this or that work. Historiography analyzes very different material. At least since the advent of critical history, the historian has claimed to do objective work, providing his readers with accurate knowledge about the past. He considers that he achieves a form of knowledge validated through historical criticism. Does this mean that the historiographer should correct the "mistakes" he thinks he encounters? We think not, as long as his discipline is defined as a branch of the sociology of knowledge.[1] To do so would mean running the risk of being anachronistic. Worse, it would presume that we have achieved a more or less definitive knowledge of the past. It would mean substituting the truth of our era, our environment, for that of previous generations.

The sociology of knowledge helps legitimize our point. Emile Durkheim, one of the pioneers in this field, held that it "cannot serve to invalidate false knowledge, 'demystify' it, or 'disalienate' it, as Marx wanted to do. . . . it is not its function to decide on the veracity of the content of knowledge, for it does not claim to take the place of epistemology. . . ."[2] Georges Gurvitch also insists that "The sociologist of knowledge must never pose the problem of the validity and value of signs, symbols, concepts, ideas, and judgments that he meets in the social reality being studied. He must only ascertain the effects of their presence, combination, and effective function."[3] In short, the purpose of the sociology of knowledge and, consequently, the sociology of historiography is first, to discover the social frameworks for knowledge that determine its content; second, to draw out the relations that exist between knowledge and the social groups or system that apprehend that knowledge through the mediation of historians; and third, in an infinitely more delicate task, to evaluate the "effective but singular causality which sometimes operates in the direction of the social frameworks' influence on the orientation and nature of knowledge; at other times in the opposite direction of knowledge's influence on the maintenance or disruption of social frameworks; and sometimes manifesting itself in reciprocal causality."[4]

Historiography obviously does not always adopt this approach. As Robert Skotheim has pointed out, there are two ways of studying the writing of history. The purpose of one is to examine methods. In this case the historiographer will stress the progress of knowledge. Changing interpretations are seen as the results of new sources used, new methods applied that were unknown to or unused by former generations of historians. The second approach uses historical writing as a source for studying the history of ideas. Interpretations are analyzed in terms of the climates of opinion and ideologies prevailing in society when the historian wrote. This approach starts from the assumption that historical knowledge is always highly relative, while the first supposes instead that it is cumulative.[5] We think the first approach is more a study of methodology. The second is, in our opinion, the only legitimate method for a sociology of historical knowledge. What this means can be indicated with an example.

A few years ago, the American historian Robin W. Winks

published a survey of Canadian historiography. Concerning French-Canadian historiography, he wrote:

From 1843 to the early 1940s French-Canadian historiography, when it ventured away from genealogy, tended to dwell upon the theme of *survivance*. Such history was polemical, not fully researched, and dogmatic, which is made only partially understandable by the fact that no professional historical training was offered in French-Canadian universities until 1945. Most of the works written prior to that time are representative of history used and abused and, while there is an occasional contribution of merit which speaks from the French language, many, such as those of Abbé Lionel-Adolphe Groulx and Jean Bruchési, often are histories for a coterie, valuable within their own framework of assumptions but mystifying and discouraging to the outsider. . . . Such works are now among the primary materials for a study of French-Canadian cultural nationalism, but they are not histories. However, Groulx's contribution is to be measured in terms of his students . . . by encouraging Robert Lionel Séguin, Michel Brunet and Guy Frégault to return to sources, he set the new generation of French-Canadian historians upon the proper path.[6]

What right does Winks have to say that our first historical works were polemical and dogmatic? What are his criteria for affirming that the works written prior to 1945 "are not histories"? To begin with, it means assuming that no good history was written before then, and this is not true. As early as the turn of the century, amateur historians like Joseph-Edmond Roy and Thomas Chapais were producing works that were to become classics.[7] They were followed by historians like Gustave Lanctot, Séraphin Marion, Paul-Emile Renaud, and Antoine Roy, all four trained in Europe, who published theses in the interwar years that compared favorably with the history being written in Europe at the time.[8] Winks is on equally weak ground when he suggests that postwar historians suddenly lost their predecessors' biases and adopted a

more neutral attitude toward history. Their work was in fact
influenced in many ways by prevailing public opinion in a
society undergoing profound changes. Lastly, when Winks
writes that sources were not used as extensively before 1945
as they were after that date, this can only mean that he is un-
acquainted with French-Canadian historiography, or at least
that part of it spanning the years from Garneau through to
the early 20th century.[9] It would be more accurate to say that
the traditional society that began to collapse in the 1940s and
1950s did not question the same things in its past as contemporary Quebec does today. This is why the prewar histories
seemed "mystifying and discouraging to the outsider." Winks
was much closer to the mark when he wrote in his introduction that "one often learns more about a people from the history they write than from the history they have made."[10] The
only way to have understood our traditional historiography
would have been to examine it in relation to the society that
produced and read it, instead of prejudging it through implicit comparisons with the standards of American society and
historiography or the work of contemporary French-Canadian
historians. With his approach, Winks has simply replaced the
subjectivity of the historians he has analyzed with his own.

Another example makes our point even clearer. A French
historian, Léo Leymarie, wrote in the 1920s that the founder
of the Notre-Dame Congregation had had an amorous adventure with Maisonneuve, the first governor of Montreal. Should
the historiographer try to determine whether the accusation is
justified? The question is in fact futile. The accusation may or
may not have been founded; the alleged adventure had no effect on Canadian destinies. The search for the "truth" may
have a certain legitimacy if the historian abandons the field of
the sociology of knowledge for that of epistemology. But the

historian seeking to understand the social frameworks of knowledge will instead note and analyze the commotion, distress,
and anxiety that Léo Leymarie's portrait of Sister Bourgeoys
provoked in Montreal.[11] There is a parallel between the resis-
tance to this version of Marguerite Bourgeoys' relations with
Maisonneuve and the reactions to Jean-Charles Harvey's *Les
demi-civilisés*, published in 1934.[12] It is precisely this resis-
tance, this reaction, that interests the sociologist of literature.
The same is true for the sociology of historical writing. It has
no business pondering whether Marcel Trudel's portrait of
Jacques Cartier as an adventurer who made strategic use of
religion to mystify the Indians is closer to the truth than Narcisse-Eutrope Dionne's 1889 account of Jacques Cartier the
evangelizing missionary; this is a false question for the sociology of knowledge. Since both authors worked from the same
basic sources, namely Cartier's account of his voyage, their
contradictory interpretations stem primarily from the authors'
different ideologies. The ultramontane Jacques Cartier of the
19th century has given way to the emancipated, secularized
Jacques Cartier of the Quiet Revolution.[13]

Of course, the evaluation of the role of great men is a choice
topic for historical relativism. There is a greater or lesser degree of relativism, depending on the object of the historical
study. As we shall see, however, biography is not the only historical genre to reflect the author's ideological environment.
Nor do we want to deny the progress in historical methods,
the additional knowledge gained thanks to new sources. On
the contrary. It can today be said that much the same progress has been made in history as in the other sciences of man.
The point is that the history of historical writing conceived as
a branch of the sociology of knowledge should not tackle
problems that belong more properly to epistemology. Such

detours are likely to lead it into serious contradictions similar
to those in which Robin Winks finds himself in discussing
French-Canadian historiography. It would be easy to list
many French-Canadian historians who like him have judged
their predecessors in the light of their own environment, their
own convictions, and their own generation.

VI. The historian as an agent of collective memory

Thus far, we have mapped the boundaries of the sociology of knowledge and the sociology of literature. Both disciplines recognize the social framework, the collective dimension, of a written work. But the analogy stops there, for history is a form of scientific knowledge and thus the contents of the historical work are supposed to faithfully represent the subject studied. It is this increasingly precise approximation of reality—always sought though never attained—that distinguishes history from fiction or poetry.

More specifically, historical knowledge is concerned with the study of former societies. This means that a sociology of historical writing must examine and classify the social frameworks of memory. Maurice Halbwachs devoted special attention to this aspect of social life. He spoke of the collective memory, on the model of the collective conscience.[1]

In his work, almost every page of which is filled with autobiographical reminiscences, Halbwachs was not primarily concerned with historical writing. He was chiefly interested in putting the oral tradition and contemporary material traces of the past into a sociological perspective.[2] In fact, he saw the collective memory as something different from and in opposition to history as written by historians.[3] It is evident, however, that when he refers to this kind of history he is thinking of factual, historicizing history, the history of the "durée courte." In general, though, his comments refer to the more highly de-

veloped forms of the historical account as well. Yet inasmuch
as it is agreed that the historian perceives the past through
the prism of the social framework of a cultural heritage, it can
be said that he becomes, by definition, the agent of the collective memory. Marc Bloch devoted a chapter of *Feudal Society*
to a discussion of memory in the great seignorial families.[4] It
is well known that these families employed professional gene-
alogists to arrange and organize the memory of the ruling
classes of the time. Similarly, the professional historian can be
described as a professional agent of the collective memory.
His role is to provide society with the coherent memory it
needs to continue its journey. Although the historian is no
longer in the service of the great families, he is still in the service of a broader community which suggests questions for him
and provides elements of interpretation. In turn, the historical
work becomes part of the collective mind and nourishes it.

Social psychology has adopted Halbwachs's pioneering approach. It is the subject of an entire chapter in a recent text-
book by Jean Stoetzel,[5] who develops the original idea by ar-
guing that as in individual growth, the evolution of groups is
accompanied by changes in memory. The collective memories
of these groups (family, religious groups, social classes, national entities, political groups, or ideological associations)
serve as a standard, an exemplary reference point. They hold
lessons for the future. Memories are retained selectively on
the basis of their meaning and usefulness for contemporary
life. This definition of how memory functions would seem to
recall Weber's thesis, repeated by Alfred Stern, to the effect
that the historian chooses the events that correspond to his
own social group's scale of values.[6] In any case, national entities are the groups closest to the notion of social memory.
Indeed, Pierre Janet demonstrated before Halbwachs that national mythologies are representations of the past in response

to the needs of the community.[7] In this sense, Western historiography acted in the 19th century—and still does today to
a certain extent—as the forger of a national conscience. More
recently, Guy Rocher has systematized Halbwachs' thinking
and again applied it to national entities:

As in the case of individuals, the past provides a community
with part of its identity. A society is defined partly by its
origins, its history, its evolution, and by certain remarkable
events. . . .
  The collective memory is not necessarily history as written
by the historians, even though it is inspired by this history.
[We might add that historians are in turn inspired by tradition.] Rather, it must simplify, summarize, prune, distort and
legendize the past; for this purpose, it often resorts to symbol-
ism. A few names of great personalities with a mythical halo
are sufficient—a few dates, a few places full of memories, and
certain events which have been more or less distorted. . . .
  Though it simplifies and distorts reality, the collective memory is nonetheless a very powerful agent of social solidarity.
The symbols that it uses are full of meaning. The memories
that are evoked by these symbols are charged with a com-
munal emotion, and they are the source of psychological communion which is almost biological. They provide an explanation of the present situation, or at least a rationalization; they
suggest lessons for the future. Thus, these symbols contribute
powerfully to the solidarity of communities, to the participa-
tion of their members, and to the orientation of individual and
collective action.[8]

It has often been said that the collective memory ideal-
izes the past. This is primarily a characteristic of the memory of national entities. It would seem that individual memory behaves this way too. Gaston Bachelard is one person
who has emphasized how adults "embellish" their memories of childhood.[9] Gilbert Durand came to the same conclusion in Les Structures anthropologiques de l'imaginaire: "The
memory . . . takes recollections and arranges them estheti-

cally. . . . Even the objectively unhappy or unfortunate childhood of a Gorky or a Stendhal cannot escape the euphemizing
enchantment of the fantastic function. The nostalgia for
childhood experiences is consubstantial with the nostalgia
for existence."[10]

It is therefore legitimate to think that the "normal" individual is almost always nostalgic about his childhood. An individual suffering from psychiatric problems, however, remem-
bers the past in a different way. "Someone who is depressed is
no longer in a condition to act," Huisman has written. "A
psyche that is exhausted, too weakened to meet the demands
of the present," lives the present "as a dream, as if it was the
past. . . . There are two ways to live the present. Either we
are ready to act, turned towards the future, and we live
events in the present. Or else we become less attentive to life,
we dream our life instead of living it, and we experience contemporary events as if they were already past."[11]

Like individual memory, social memory can discredit the
past, just as it can enhance it. In the words of Raymond
Aron: "The consciousness of history varies with peoples and
times; now it is dominated by nostalgia for the past, now by
the feeling of preservation or hope concerning the future.
These fluctuations are easily understood. Certain peoples ex-
pect greatness, others preserve the memory of it, some feel
linked with a tradition they wish to prolong, others are eager
for novelty, thirsting for liberty and forgetfulness. . . . Neither
the optimism of progress nor the pessimism of separation and
solitude define properly the historical idea."[12]

The historian's history conforms to these different tendencies in varying degrees. They can give rise to a portrait of the
past as either a golden age or a time of poverty and misery. It
all depends on the vision of society that underlies the histori-

cal interpretation. The romantic school, and nationalist historiography in general, has thus tended to see the past as a
lost Eldorado. The dream of paradise lost? A rejection of the
dreariness of the present? Nationalist historiography can be
said to be a people's nostalgia for its childhood, analogous to
an individual's nostalgia for his early years. National entities
tend to enhance the exploits and great men in their past. The
Germans' silence about their history during the immediate
postwar period was no coincidence. It was imposed by their
contemporary shame. Concerned with rebuilding the coun-
try, afflicted with feelings of guilt, German historians did not
seem to have anything good or pleasing to say to their com-
patriots.[13]

Generally speaking, the conservative ideologies that advo-
cate a return to the past or the preservation of a heritage
from it give rise to an idealized depiction of the past. To
Trevor-Roper, who wrote that a historian "ought to love the
past," Carr, with his optimistic, progressive philosophy of history, replied: "To love the past may easily be an expression of
the nostalgic romanticism of old men and old societies, a
symptom of loss of faith and interest in the present or the
future."[14]

A society that shows signs of losing its vitality, that does
not control its future, that is anxious about it, will tend to
look back to its past. It will tend to live like an old man who
looks to the past because the life left before him is almost
over. "All that was once before me is now behind me—my future has become the past," wrote the historian Benjamin
Sulte in his old age.[15] R. S. Lynd wrote: "Elderly people in
our culture are frequently oriented towards the past, the time
of their vigor and power, and resist the future as a threat. It
is probable that a whole culture in an advanced stage of loss

of relative power and disintegration may thus have a dominant orientation towards a lost golden age, while life is lived
sluggishly along in the present."[16]

But although the past evoked in some cases may be crowned
with a halo of glory and more or less legendary exploits, the
collective memory can also retain a derogatory image of the
past, preserving its ugliness, suffering, and alienating features.
This happens when happiness is in the future, when the future is seen as a march toward the millennium. This is how
progressive philosophers of history, like those of the Enlightenment and today's Marxists, see the past. It is downgraded to
the advantage of some future happiness, a liberation yet to
come. French romantic historiography played this role in part,
in order to consolidate the advances of the French Revolution.[17] Any discussion of contradictory reconstructions of the
past brings to mind the two versions of the British Conquest—
the Conquest as a fortunate event, in traditional French-
Canadian histories; and the Conquest as catastrophe, in neo-
nationalist histories. The former belonged to a society turned
in on itself, fearing change; while the latter, the Conquest as
a permanent misfortune, is part of a strategy of decolonization.[18] In short, the historian's thinking reflects the hope for a
future paradise or the disappointment at the loss of a former
golden age of his contemporaries, be they a people or some
broader cultural entity.

VII. The historian as Ideologue

We have made frequent reference to ideologies in the scholarly historical process. If, as Gurvitch has written, "Historical truth is the most ideological of all scientific truths," it is worth examining the meaning of the term ideology.[1]

The collective memory simplifies and distorts. Its role is to stimulate a sense of belonging, of social solidarity. It carries an intense emotional charge designed to bring the members of a community together around certain symbols. It explains a situation and suggests an "orientation of individual and collective action." Are not these the characteristics of nationalist ideology? The collective memory brings us to a consideration of historical thought as ideology.

Ideology, Fernand Dumont has written, is "both an element of the situation and a dynamic plan for action." It is a *representation* of a social *entity* from a perspective of action *in* and *on* society."[2] Drawing in part on various writings by Dumont, Rocher has defined ideology as "a system of ideas and judgments which are explicit and generally organized; which serve to describe, explain, interpret or justify the situation of a group or community; and which, largely on the basis of values, suggest a precise orientation to the historical action of this group or collectivity."[3] In its temporal dimension, we can already see that ideology is a reality in many respects similar to the historian's approach. Dumont has himself drawn the parallel between ideology and historical knowledge. This is how he puts it: "Starting always from the present-day situation, the historian sometimes pays special attention to a situation in the past that seems to him especially meaningful and related in some way to problems and hopes of the present."[4] He added, "Men produce ideologies—including historical research, at times—to find some justification, a certain legitimate stability, for their existence in societies where the present tends to create anxiety."[5]

VIII.   History as the science of time

To what extent do the characteristic features of ideology apply—albeit in varying degrees—to historical knowledge? To answer this question, we should begin by saying that history is the science of time, just as geography is the science of space. And the notion of time inherently links the present, the past, and the future. Bergson, and subsequently Heidegger, were two philosophers who recognized the necessary link between these three dimensions of temporality.[1] For Heidegger, history was, so to speak, a projection of the future into the past. This affirmation has not failed to raise the ire of the "objectivists." Paul Veyne saw in it the ambition to "dignify nationalist historiography of the 19th century as an intellectualist philosophy."[2] A number of others, however, acknowledge the legitimacy of Heidegger's thesis.

As a general rule, Aron argues that man looks "spontaneously for precedents in the past" in order to "situate the present moment in an evolving future."[3] In commenting on Marxist ideology, he applies this general proposition to the study of the past, writing that the "concrete interpretations of the past are bound up with wills reaching out to the future."[4] According to Aron, "The historian, in so far as he lives historically, has a tendency to action and seeks the past pertaining to his future."[5] The present, "being incomplete, is determined with reference to the future, imagined and unknown by the men who are destined to create it."[6] This is why, for Aron, "the future reveals the truth about the past only bit by bit, never de-

43

finitively."[7] This dialectical relationship between the past, the present, and the future is what ultimately explains an observation often repeated by Aron: "Each age chooses its own past, drawing from the collective treasure; each new life transfigures the heritage it has received, giving it another future and imparting to it another meaning."[8] By its very nature, historical research "expresses a dialogue between the present and the past, in which the present takes and keeps the initiative."[9]

History as the science of the present, indeed of the future? The mere idea is sure to raise more than a few eyebrows among objectivists. Marrou did not accept the extreme positions put forward by Croce and Aron.[10] In England, Elton attacked Carr for recognizing that historical knowledge has a futuristic dimension and for identifying it with the ideology of progress.[11]

The conception, espoused by Carr and other relativists, of history as the science of the present and indeed the future owes much to the thinking of Benedetto Croce, who was one of the first in the 20th century to recognize the contemporary dimension of historical work. Croce gave this explanation:

What constitutes history may thus be described: it is the act of comprehending and understanding induced by the requirements of practical life. . . . Historical works of all times and of all peoples have come to birth in this manner and always will be born like this, out of fresh requirements which arise, and out of the perplexities involved in these. We shall not understand the history of men and of other times unless we ourselves are alive to the requirements which that history satisfied. . . .[12]

Applied to national history, this statement confirms once again that an understanding of historical writing cannot be divorced from an understanding of the milieu and the aspirations of the age that produced it. Croce applied his theory of historical knowledge to Michelet:

Michelet's *History of France* [is marked by a] fantastic idolization of France as a physical, intellectual, and moral person, with her own private genius and mission in the world, whose present and past may be interrogated for the revelation of her future. It certainly cannot be denied that with this fanciful theme there are interwoven original and acute historical judgments arising out of moral and political problems, which Michelet treated with a profound and noble zeal confirmed by the whole tenor of his life.[13]

When Dumont evokes the enigmas and anxieties of the present, is he really all that far removed from Croce, who saw the story of history as the story of liberty?[14] Historians today object to this on the grounds that although the purpose of history in the 19th century may have been to provide lessons for the future, this is no longer the case, especially since nationalist history has given way to other forms of historical writing. It is true that the 19th-century historian was conscious of the futuristic aspect of his work. English historians provide numerous examples of this. Thomas Carlyle (1795-1881), for instance, wrote that the past was "the true fountain of knowledge; by whose light alone, consciously or unconsciously, can the Present and the Future be interpreted and guessed at."[15] For Henry Thomas Buckle (1821-1862), "there must always be a connexion between the way in which men contemplate the past, and the way in which they contemplate the present."[16] Lord Acton (1834-1902), said: "As each age, so its view of the Past. . . . False notion of history gives a false color to present time."[17] A French historian, Gabriel Hanotaux, described the historian as "someone who sees into the future."[18] There is no lack of such testimonies from a former age, but many of today's professional historians confirm, implicitly if not explicitly, the contemporary nature and indeed the anticipatory aspect of historical knowledge.

It would be superfluous to include further quotations here. There is, however, a distinction that should be made. Some historians emphasize the capacity of historical science to predict the future course of events. They consider this stems from the objectivity of the historical account which comes to reflect reality more and more accurately with improvements in historical method and with additional, more varied sources. It is probably this conviction that motivated Robert Mandrou to write in his preface to Fernand Ouellet's *Economic and Social History of Quebec, 1760-1850* that "whoever is interested in the future of French Canada, whoever seeks to understand the Quebec of the 1960s, must read this book."[19] The book is intended to be a contribution toward "a better knowledge of the Canadian past, which is indispensable for the understanding of a present dimly perceived and fraught with critical choices."[20] In contrast, though, when Sir Lewis Namier made the paradoxical comment that "historians imagine the past and remember the future,"[21] he came across clearly as a relativist. Boyd C. Shafer was even more explicit when he wrote recently: "As long as men hope they will debate the nature of the past, for their differing hopes depend, in part at least, upon their differing understandings of their experience, just as the differing understandings they reach depend, in part at least, upon the nature of their differing hopes."[22] Richard Hofstadter was just as relativist in his conclusion about the progressive historians: "At their best, the interpretative historians have gone to the past with some passionate concern for the future."[23]

These assertions have, of course, been criticized by some historians. Marrou, for example, disagreed with Aron's statement that history was past, present, and future.[24] But others have been more willing to accept the relativist view. As a whole, the New Left historians in the United States have echoed Becker's acknowledgment that "every generation, our own included, will, must inevitably, understand the past and anticipate the future in the light of its own restricted experience."[25] They have also endorsed Beard's observations that history "had to do with molding the future rather than understanding the past."[26]

These comments from historians should suffice, although we could also cite Georges Lefebvre, Léon Halkin, Walsh, Butterfield and Carr,[27] and undoubtedly many others as well if we had studied contemporary authors more extensively. They would all agree that historical knowledge is intertwined with society's prospects and hopes for the future. The historian may transpose his hopes into a committed interpretation of the past (the subjectivist thesis), or the accuracy of his research may shed light on man's choices (the objectivist thesis). In either case, the nature of the historical inquiry remains the same: an exploration in time whereby the future and the past are molded by the present. And since the present is constantly changing and evolving, the historical memory is always changing too.

IX. History as choice

Because history is the science of elapsed time, because it interprets a situation, traces its origins, and implicitly
or explicitly proposes an orientation for action, we can agree
that it is not unrelated to the structure of ideology. We will
now look at how history, or more broadly the historical production of a given milieu and era, like ideology, simplifies and
distorts all of the past in various ways. In doing so, history re-
inforces its resemblance to ideology.

In theory, the historian is interested in all of human experience. Fernand Dumont concluded on the question of whether
history is ideology: "The oldest cliché in historical thinking
sums up the discussion best: really writing history means
taking an interest in the *multiplicity* of past events in and for
themselves." This was how a historian could be objective, he
said.[1] In practice, however, historical knowledge is the result
of a series of choices. Besides being selective, the historian applies criteria of arrangement and importance, as they are re-
ferred to in the historical method. What does this mean?

When a historian chooses to study a very specifically defined period of time or geographical area, or when he does
research on a very limited topic, his choices are governed by
determining factors—whether objectivists like it or not.[2] The
historian's free choice, as Chaïm Pérelman pointed out, leads
him to embrace ideological concerns.[3] Consequently, historians
pay more or less attention to certain periods of history or certain aspects of human behavior, depending on the concerns of

their contemporaries. Thus, for instance, the recent transition from history dominated by political and religious themes to predominantly economic history in Quebec society is closely related to the increasingly secular nature of that society. This does not mean that there are no other contributing factors in this evolution. It is clearly partly the result of the postwar professionalization of the historian in Quebec and his growing contacts with the history written in other countries. But in the final analysis, new approaches, questions, and methods were imported as a result of the collapse of traditional society. The relationship between the new Quebec society and the new historical writing is just as significant as were the explicit value judgments of past historians. It is this relationship that is the subject matter of the sociology of historical knowledge. In the end, both the methodological progress and the growing volume of documentation available have less effect on the contents of this knowledge than do the major issues and problems in the historian's environment, and from which he can never be entirely detached. His milieu suggests fields of study for the historian that bear some connection to the concerns of his contemporaries. This is what Raymond Aron meant when he wrote that "historical or sociological researches are connected with extra-scientific intentions."[4] The American progressive historians, who are rightly seen as the pioneers of the sociology of knowledge, have carried the recognition of the inevitably subjective nature of the historian's choice very far. For Charles Beard:

He (the historian) may edit documents, although there are perils in the choice of documents to be edited and in any case the choice of documents will bear some reference to an interpretation of values and importance-subjective considerations. To avoid this difficulty, the historian may confine his attention to some very remote and microscopic area of time and place, such as the price of cotton in Alabama between 1850 and

1860. . . . But even then the historian would be a strange creature if he never asked himself why he regarded these matters as worthy of his labor and love, or why society provides a living for him during his excursions and explorations.[5]

Once a historian has chosen to study a given period, theme or place (be it a town or city or an international cultural area), he inevitably discards a certain amount of documentation. His criterion in choosing what to keep and what to reject is the importance of the material; and any evaluation of its importance is in turn associated with a value judgment. His judgment of the importance of something reflects interests, beliefs and values that he cannot keep separate from the act of knowledge.[6]

The relativist theory of historical knowledge has recognized in various ways the connotations of value involved in the historian's choice between what is essential and what is incidental, what is important and necessary, and what is superfluous and useless. It has been argued, for example, that the historian substitutes his own scale of values for that of the period he studies. But the two are not equally valid, for the simple reason that the historian is acquainted with the future of the past he is studying (a future he anticipates if his field is contemporary history).

Georges Lefebvre is one of the historians who have recognized the subjectivity of the historian's choice. The historian writes on the basis of "what subsists from the past."[7] History is choice as well because it records the facts "worth remembering."[8] Lefebvre concluded: "It is easy to understand that the social frameworks of memory have as much influence on the choice of the facts that retain our attention in history."[9] Gottschalk argues that any historical inquiry, regardless of whether it is guided by a working hypothesis, involves a value judgment at the point when the historian determines what is important: "We are forced to the conclusion that the decision as to what is relevant is largely subjective."[10] The same is true, in his opinion, of the amount and relative importance of the space allotted for recounting the various facts.[11]

No need to insist. The quantitative analysis of contents has demonstrated the ideological significance of the relative amounts of space given to a set of facts, themes or problems in the press. A newspaper does not report everything that happens from one day or one edition to the next; nor does history, and in particular syntheses—works conceived as surveys of entire periods or regions. Similarly, overall historical production for one period in a given milieu does not make use of all the information to be found in the total documentary record. Thus, as Carr observed: "The historian is necessarily selective. The belief in a hard core of historical facts existing objectively and independently of the interpretation of the historian is preposterous fallacy."[12]

Take the case of a synthesis. Here the amount of space assigned to various figures, periods, events, lifestyles and achievements of civilization reflects a concern to trace the highlights, the major and significant aspects of historical evolution. The importance attributed to the various figures and events, etc., corresponds to a scale of values. Is the work a biography (a form that some hesitate to acknowledge as part of the historical discipline)?[13] The choice of the subject of the biography is already an ideological decision. Cameron Nish has capably demonstrated that the predilection of English-Canadian historians for Henri Bourassa in recent years is not unrelated to the equally recent enthusiasm for creating the bilingual, bicultural Canada advocated by Bourassa half a century ago. Bourassa's popularity, Nish has remarked, represents a kind of canonization by English Canada of a French Canadian in the hope of cementing the union of the founding peoples of

Canada.[14] The same can perhaps be said of Marcel Trudel's *Chiniquy*.[15] Published in the mid-1950s, it reflected the spirit of the struggle waged by *Cité libre* to shatter Quebec's Christendom. The prolific biographer Sir Lewis Namier submitted to psychoanalysis; there would perhaps be much to be learned from the psychoanalysis of contemporary biographers.

Is the work a monograph on a limited period, concerned with studying a specific aspect of the total reality? The very choice of the period, event, or theme is an indication of the writer's ideological approach. For a long time French Canada favored the study of the French regime; today this tendency is being reversed. The above mentioned pattern is related to the conservative evolution of French Canada which persisted until recent years and the subsequent Quiet Revolution, which was accompanied by greater curiosity about the more immediate past of French-Canadian society. Quebec historians today are interested in the history of the French-Canadian bourgeoisie, while traditional historiography was more interested in the nobility—a development not unrelated to the decline of the values of the *ancien regime* in Quebec. Nor is it unrelated to the realization of the underdevelopment of Quebec society. All this points clearly to an intimate link between the author and his public, between ideological production and historical production. Similarly, if in coming years North America emphasizes Amerindian history, this will not be unrelated to the rejection of post-industrial capitalist society by a sizeable segment of the young generation eager for a return to primitive society.

Finally, in assessing the historical output of a given milieu as a whole its predominant tendencies may be ascribed to ideology. For instance, the emergence of a left-wing school of historical writing in English Canada is intimately related to a growing radicalism in Canada. In 1967 26 percent of the theses on English-Canadian history in progress in Canadian universities dealt with one aspect or another of the left. In this case, it is not hard to see the connection between the milieu and the choice of thesis subjects in history.[16]

My observations, it should be noted, do not imply that the historical inquiry is pursued in an overtly partial way, and the sociology of historical writing proposed by Febvre and taken up by Alfred Dubuc[17] does not presume that partiality is inevitable. Certainly, a sociology of 19th-century historical writing would have no difficulty in identifying and classifying the explicit judgments of the historians. But 20th-century historiography provides numerous examples of historians who are remarkably detached. Nonetheless, we may conclude that historical objectivity has its limits.

X. The present limits of historical objectivity: The role of the public and of pluralist explanations

Narrative or descriptive history, with its emphasis on important, striking, or unique individuals and events, can be practiced today with a sincere attempt at detachment. The historian's professional conscience means that when he investigates a subject, he will not hesitate to consult all available sources; he will criticize personal accounts, using the discoveries of experimental psychology; and when he finds a discordant version of the facts, he will carefully weigh its value. He will use official information, that is, the source known at the time of the event, and compare and contrast it with documents then kept secret, in which the historical actors confided their thinking and motives, and which thus reveal the background for the decisions made. If certain conditions are satisfied, he will perhaps be able to discover the "truth" about the event in question. But to do so, he must begin by putting aside his personal preferences. He may like or dislike this or that historical figure because he appreciates or abhors certain of his characteristics, but these emotional reactions must not influence the history he writes. His national and social background must not intrude either. Nor may he allow himself to be seduced by any philosophy of history or any theory of historical interpretation.[1] Supposing that this ideal historian existed—and there are many who would doubt it possible—his work would ultimately still contain unavoidable traces of subjectivity in its relationship to its public.

A recent book, *Quebec sous la loi des mesures de guerre 1918*,[2] was apparently written "with the utmost objectivity"—or so Fernand Dumont tells us in his preface.[3] For the purposes of this discussion, we can suppose that this is indeed the case. It is nevertheless true that the book would never have had the impact it had on the public in Quebec if the latter had not lived through the events and changes that culminated in the historic October crisis of 1970. Without Jean Provencher's book, an editorialist for *Le Devoir* would probably never have thought of drawing a parallel between the Irish crisis and "the deaths in the first conscription crisis in Quebec."[4] Whether he likes it or not, the historian's history is used for non-scientific purposes, for which he bears some responsibility—however much he might prefer to wash his hands of it.

To come back to something said in a previous chapter: a work is inseparable from the public that reads it. In the end, this is why it is inevitably contemporary. In ten or twenty years, Provencher's book will by no means elicit the same emotional response from the public that made it a successful work at publication. Unless Quebec experiences another situation comparable to that of the fall of 1970, the book will never again fully meet the expectations of an audience that will never be the same again, because it evolves with time. If the television programs of the 1950s were broadcast today, the material content of the programs would be the same as they were several decades ago, but the dialogue established between the programs and a new public would change their content, their meaning, substantially. They would be transformed—rethought, Croce would say—by an audience whose outlook and reactions have changed, for the dialogue between the present and the past is itself a historical phenomenon.

The preceding example shows where historical relativism inevitably and invariably comes in. Ideally, there might be no subjectivity in the work itself; yet, the very choice of the subject necessarily bears some relationship to the present. Thus the conscription crisis and the October crisis. Even if there was originally no subjectivity in the historical inquiry, it is undeniably present in its extension to the public. Interpretation of the human past cannot be compared to the physicist's research. Applied to either the historian or his public, Walsh's quip is most telling here: "I am assuming," he wrote about historical knowledge in relation to natural sciences, "that 'Soviet' biology and 'bourgeois' physics are nonexistent."[5]

In practice, the historian can achieve a degree of detachment in studying the past comparable to that of his colleagues in the other social sciences—insofar as his approach resembles theirs. He can then write with as much precision as any sociologist, demographer, psychologist, or even economist can in an empirical study. Need we recall that with the emergence of the newer social sciences, there were thinkers who enriched historical method with some fruitful borrowing? Karl Lamprecht (1856-1915) in Germany, James Harvey Robinson (1863-1936) in the United States and Henri Berr (1863-1954) and François Simiand in France[6] all contributed in their own ways to the osmosis between history and its neighboring disciplines. The osmosis has been so extensive that contemporary historical theory has as much recourse to recent auxiliary sciences as it does to all the traditional auxiliary sciences—more concerned with sources than with methods.[7] History has become a genuine science of man. We now have to show how the past is still subject to ideological interpretations.

Increasingly refined analytical techniques have meant that this new history can be somewhat inaccurately termed scientific:[8] it studies groups instead of individuals; it takes a quantitative approach to the many facets of reality, from economy and demography to lifestyles and the cycles of the *longue duree* [long term or long time span] and it examines structures and conjunctures ["stillness and movement"] that do indeed allow us to perceive more fully the shape of former societies. But this does not mean that relativism has been banished from historical scholarship nor that it is now pertinent merely to the choice of subjects and the audience addressed (more usually specialists). The causal explanation is still largely bound by ideological constraints (true mainly in the case of an event with a number of causes).[9] For even today the science of history has not yet succeeded—will it ever?—in sorting out the relative importance of the many causal factors. Look at an example from Fernand Ouellet's work.

In his *Histoire économique et sociale du Québec*,[10] Ouellet argues that the explosion of anger in 1837 resulted from an agricultural crisis, demographic pressures, overcrowding in the liberal professions, and so on. In short, a series of economic and social imbalances were at the root of the exacerbated nationalism that eventually led to armed clashes. Very good. But how decisive was each factor in this social upheaval? Was there an overriding factor that determined all the others? The nationalist argument has tried to work back to a first cause, the Conquest, seeing all the subsequent imbalances as a consequence of that event. As a matter of fact, perhaps the disappearance of the French-Canadian entrepreneur three or four decades after the Conquest can be partly explained as a result of an unequal competition in which the merchants of British origin, at an advantage over their French-Canadian rivals in the import sector, won out. If this is the case, how legitimate is it to blame, as Ouellet does, the disappearance of the French-Canadian bourgeoisie on the community's incapacity to generate genuine entrepreneurship? By the end of the late 19th century, the *coureurs de bois* and the French-Canadian loggers who replaced them had become laborers for British entrepreneurs. But is not this phenomenon of ethnic proletarianization, observed by Lord Durham, in turn a result of the Conquest? French Canadians tended to fall back on retail trade, the liberal professions and agriculture. Was this not another delayed effect of the annexation of New France by the British Empire? Nor could the demographic pressures be explained by a shortage of land alone, as Ouellet implies. The near-monopolization of Eastern Townships land by a handful of speculators and the creation of clergy and Crown reserves were equally important factors. So goes the basic outline of the nationalist interpretation of the century that followed the Conquest.[11]

The objection previously raised remains pertinent. To what extent was the Conquest the cause of the imbalances that led to the rebellion? What was the relative influence of each of the consequences stemming from the first cause in the overall evolution of French-Canadian society up until armed revolt broke out? These questions are not about to be answered. Listing the factors involved is obviously more fruitful than reciting the acts of the great men seen as the links in the chain of cause and effect in the purely political interpretations of the period. But unless and until we can weigh the importance of each variable involved, the explanation remains, to a large extent, a matter of ideologies. Unable to achieve a laboratory replica of the evolution of the period and isolate certain variables to ascertain their influence, the historian has to fall back largely on his background and beliefs, nourishing the explanation with his convictions, sympathies, and emotions. "Even the historian most concerned with objectivity," Jan Crayebeck has written, "concludes that the cause is what seems most plausible to him in the context of the era in which he lives, his milieu, his class (whose preconceptions he often shares), his intellectual personality, etc."[12]

XI. The limits of objectivity in the social sciences

In comparison with the achievements of the natural sciences, the approximations in the social sciences are still largely associated with ideologies. Both subject and object of his inquiry, man cannot be totally objective. Will he eventually succeed in identifying more exactly the nature and importance of the factors that determine his social life? He will certainly not be able to ignore human free will, also responsible for what is in all likelihood an imposing number of historical events that cannot be explained by the laws of human behavior.

It should not be forgotten that the quantitative approach and statistical explanations, with their seductive certitudes, have their limits in both history and the social sciences as a whole. Indeed, in his thesis on the limits of historical objectivity, Aron made no distinction between the approach of someone like Simiand and that of someone like Durkheim.[1] He repeatedly points out certain very weak interpretations in Durkheim's analysis of suicide.

Not enough work has been done on the parallels in the development of history and the other social sciences. More often than not, sociologists or philosophers have reflected on the nature of historical inquiry. Yet some self-criticism on both sides would not be out of place. Sociology is the daughter of history and, like history, it had a theological age with pioneers like

Buchez.[2] Similarly, was the moralizing sociology of Tourville and Desmolins really all that different from the lessons then provided by nationalist history? Comte's positivism had much the same influence on Durkheim as it had on the historical school of Langlois and Seignobos. Despite the conflicts between the former and the latter, the methods of both disciplines were imbued with the same scientific intention.[3] Their shared concern with ridding knowledge of all metaphysics and philosophy speaks volumes about how closely they are related. It can only be hoped that eventually the sociological approach to knowledge will be extended and applied to the analysis of more than the science of history. History is merely one of many disciplines generally governed by the ideological trends of an era. In this respect, Alfred Dubuc's remark is worth pondering: "Social science, because it is the science of man, cannot escape the problem of values . . . . the danger with the scientific approach is to pretend not to recognize this. The only way to solve the problem is not to discard the values, but rather to try to be constantly aware of our own values, to see them objectively. Indeed, there cannot be a historical science without a sociology of history and historians."[4]

In distinguishing between history as knowledge and history as ideology, Dubuc reiterated this theme:

Actually, ideology is to the social sciences what the creative imagination is to mathematics.

Anyone who claims to be free from ideology . . . is refusing to recognize the values everyone has. He deludes himself and deludes others. As a matter of fact, the notion of the end of ideologies is the most ideological notion of all. For it excludes the use of any critical approach and thereby opposes the development of science. In terms of political action, it becomes the most insidious and thus the most effective defense of the established order.

. . . Ideology is the yeast of knowledge.[5]

Fernand Dumont, who has himself often stressed the ideological nature of historical knowledge, has written: "We can no longer retreat from the possibility of a sociology of sociology."[6] He evokes the inevitable ideological constraints that no sociologist can completely immunize himself against, even should he wish to:

When he studies economic or demographic facts, the sociologist certainly feels confronted with a difficult building job, but he can at least think that he is confronted with realities that are distinct from his own consciousness. All such illusions are quickly dispelled when he is studying cultural phenomena: here each fact has the ambiguous status of both object and explanation of the object. How can the sociologist in turn explain without assuming the very way in which this object records and reveals his own existence?[7]

If we look at the kinds of history practiced nowadays by historians, we reach the same conclusions. Economic history and historical demography willingly lay claim to a certain degree of precision. Intellectual history, the history of collective psychology—in short, cultural history—is more difficult to treat with quantitative approaches and is thus less categorical. There is, of course, a whole range of degrees of inferences, depending on how distant the period studied by the historian is. But in all cases, knowledge is a fundamental relation between the subject who apprehends and the object of his knowledge.

In the study of societies as a whole, the sociologist encounters the same snares that await the author of historical surveys. This is what the sociologist has to say about them:

When the sociologist or anthropologist seeks to express a general interpretation of a society, he runs up against the major ideologies of the milieu involved. Before we ever begin to work out the science of a society, the society has already acquired its own coherent vision of what it is. . . . One of the

consequences of this situation is that there is inevitably a con-
tinuity between the dominant ideologies of a milieu and any
scientific interpretation of a whole society. At times the interpretation will be simply an explanation and systematization of
these ideologies; often it will represent a challenge to them
bearing with it demands and value judgments. We would
accord ourselves a kind of *deus ex machina* objectivity should
we forget or ignore this very concrete, though cumbersome,
condition of the emergence of any general sociology. There is
thus a sort of underlying polemic involved in any broad sociological interpretation of a total society.

The words are those of a sociologist familiar with the philosophy and sociology of knowledge. Dumont continues:

To get around this problem, it has sometimes been suggested
that only a stranger can properly interpret a society as a
whole. The solution is very fragile, in my opinion: a certain
identification with the object is both inevitable and necessary
in our sciences; as long as we do not have the techniques
needed to measure or mete out this identification, removing
the scientist from his usual surroundings cannot be a decisive
solution for the problem before us. This is all the more true to
the extent that a foreign sociologist, in order to grasp the
object of his study, would have to make use of the major
local works or at the very least compare and contrast them
with his own explanation.[8]

There are numerous examples in the historical and sociological writing of French Canada that could be used to illustrate Dumont's comments.[9] Instead, look at how his thinking
would apply to other kinds of researchers.

We have argued that the historian is always "present-
minded." This means that his history involves an underlying
or explicit comparison with the present. The same could be
said of the sociologist: when he studies the mechanisms, functioning, and values of traditional society, he always does so
in relation to the changes wrought by industrial society. The
sociologist who studies underdevelopment proceeds in the

same way. Whether he likes it or not, his approach includes a set of implicit or explicit references to what is called developed society. In doing so, he embraces a set of values belonging to developed society. If, on the contrary, he sees weaknesses or shortcomings in that society, he will implicitly or explicitly put Western industrial society on trial. It would seem superfluous to add that the historian, in his own chronological perspective, is always inevitably confronted with the need to back up his arguments with more or less explicit value judgments.

To put it unambiguously: all knowledge is ideological and/or inspired by ideologies and/or contributes to the emergence or helps sustain ideologies in a social environment. This is partly due to methodological shortcomings, but it also stems from the fact that the language of the social sciences is accessible to the public at large.

That is why a sociology of knowledge must try as best it can to retrace the ideology both in the choice of the subject to be studied and the historical work itself, and in its extension to its public. The readers (the audience), are partly responsible for the content of the work. Chaïm Pérelman, who has seriously contemplated the notion of audience in both the specifically ideological discourse and in the scientific presentation,[10] has come to the conclusion that it is a decisive factor in the historian's choice.[11] Thus no historical inquiry, from the most "exact" to the most explicitly subjective, can be excluded from the sociology of knowledge. In this respect, refusing to recognize the relative nature of knowledge amounts to claiming to write in a specialist's jargon incomprehensible to the layman. Yet, until there is further proof to the contrary, the most detached historian, backing up his attempt at objectivity with the most rigorous methods, still exerts an influence on the public at large, by whom his work is continuously assessed. Here we reach the ultimate limits of knowledge. Refusing to recognize these limits amounts to wanting to make the social sciences something sacred in the eyes of the profane non-specialist. No need to insist. The great historians of our time are very glad that the ordinary man of the 20th century knows something of their work. This does not necessarily mean that the results of historical inquiry have no scientific value. It would be absurd to refuse to recognize that history provides a certain approximation of reality. It is obvious enough that the historian does not dream up his tale without reference to, or respect for, the primary documentary data. It is nonetheless true that each era has its own truths that it projects into the future. The historian's scientific curiosity is in turn guided, albeit in varying degrees, by the concerns of his contemporaries.

In short, wherever we turn—to psychology, sociology, philosophy or theology—we are repeatedly reminded that the dream of happiness and the absolute that humanity has always cherished has its roots in how man sees his past. In search of paradise lost or new kingdoms to conquer, the historical conscience is inseparable from the ambitions, desires, inhibitions and frustrations experienced by the historian and his *audience*.

Notes

Introduction

1. Goethe, quoted by E. H. Carr in *What is History?* (New York, 1967), p. 165.
2. J. G. A. Pocock, *The Ancient Constitution and the Feudal Law: A Study in English Historical Thought in the Seventeenth Century* (New York, 1967: a reprint of the 1957 edition); see the introduction.
3. These remarks are based on an examination of the work by B. G. Reizov, *L'historiographie romantique française, 1815-1830* (Moscow, n.d.).
4. Adam Schaff, *Histoire et vérité: Essai sur l'objectivité de la connaissance historique* (Paris, 1971), pp. 190-201, 305ff; published in English as *History and Truth* (New York, 1976).
5. Felix Gilbert, "Intellectual History: its Aims and Methods," *Daedalus* (Winter 1971), pp. 80-97.

Chapter I

1. Fernand Dumont, "La fonction sociale de l'histoire," *Histoire sociale*, no. 4 (November 1969), pp. 5-16; see p. 15.
2. This refers in particular to the work of Henri Beaudé, Camille Roy, Emile Chartier and the Canon Robitaille. Frégault, at least in the early part of his career, and Lanctôt, took an interest in this. Philippe Sylvain and Father Thomas Charland have also written good articles on the subject. Usually, however, the authors have simply replaced the biases of the historians they analyzed with their own.
3. Pierre de Grandpré, *Histoire de la littérature française du Québec*, 4 vols. (Montreal, 1967-69).
4. Guy Palmade, *L'Histoire, Coll. U.* (Paris, 1971), p. 5ff.
5. See the Comité français des sciences historiques, *La recherche historique en France de 1940 à 1945* (Paris, 1965), p. ix.
6. Raymond Aron, *Introduction à la philosophie de l'histoire: Essai sur les limites de l'objectivité historique* (Paris, 1967), p. 356; published in English as *Introduction to the Philosophy of History: An Essay on the Limits of Historical Objectivity*, trans. George J. Irwin (Boston, 1961).
7. Lucien Febvre, *Combats pour l'Histoire*, 2nd ed. (Paris, 1965), p. 437.
8. Philippe Wolff, "L'étude des économies et des sociétés avant l'ère

statistique," in C. Samaran, *L'Histoire et ses méthodes,* Coll. "Encyclopédie de la Pléiade" (Paris, 1961).

9. Lucien Febvre, *op. cit.,* p. 438.

10. Charles Morazé, *Trois essais sur histoire et culture* (Paris, 1948),
foreword, p. vii.

11. Alphonse Dupront, "L'Histoire après Freud," *Revue de l'Enseignement supérieur,* no. 44-45 (1969), p. 44.

12. However, the new collection "Dossiers Clio," published by the
Presses universitaires de France, reflects a more receptive attitude
towards relativism.

13. Fernand Dumont, *op. cit.,* p. 13.

14. W. H. Walsh, *Philosophy of History* (New York and Evanston,
1968), pp. 179ff.

15. Paul Veyne, "Statut scientifique de l'histoire," *Encyclopaedia Univer-
salis,* vol. 8 (1970), in the article "Histoire." By the same author, see
also *Comment on écrit l'Histoire* (Paris, 1971). Raymond Aron's
reply is also worth reading: "Comment l'historien écrit l'épistémol-
ogie: à propos d'un livre de Paul Veyne," *Annales–Economies–
Sociétés–Civilisation* (AESC) (November 1971), pp. 1319-1354.

16. Jean Glénisson, in *La recherche historique en France de 1940 à 1945,*
op. cit., pp. lff and lxiii.

17. Boyd C. Shafer, ed., *Historical Study in the West* (New York, 1968).

18. *Ibid.,* p. 65.

19. J. Momsen, "The Development of Scholarly Historical Study in Western Germany," in *Historical Study in the West,* pp. 126ff.

20. G. R. Elton, *Modern Historians and British History 1485-1945: A
Critical Bibliography 1945-1969* (London, 1970). British social his-
tory has some striking similarities with the French school. See H. J.
Perkins, "Social History," in H. P. R. Finbert, ed., *Approaches to
History: a Symposium* (London, 1962), pp. 51-82.

21. Carr, *op. cit.,* p. 71.

22. *Ibid.,* p. 72.

23. Benedetto Croce, *History as the Story of Liberty* (London, 1941);
and *Theory and History of Historiography* (London, 1921).

24. On Collingwood's debt to Croce, see *The Idea of History* (New York,
1968), pp. 190-204.

25. Collingwood, *ibid.,* pp. 231-249.

26. *Ibid.,* pp. 245ff.

27. *Ibid.,* p. 233.

28. W. H. Walsh, *op. cit.,* pp. 22ff; Henri-I. Marrou, *De la connaissance
historique* (Paris, 1954), pp. 231 and 295ff., published in English as
The Meaning of History (Baltimore, 1966); Léon-E. Halkin, *Elé-
ments de critique historique* (Liège, 1966), p. 27; S. E. Morison,
quoted in Thomas N. Guinsberg, *The Dimensions of History* (Chicago, 1971), p. 1.

29. N.-E. Dionne, *Samuel de Champlain,* 2 vol. (Quebec City, 1906),
vol. 2, p. 242; Joseph-Edmond Roy, *Le Baron de Lahontan* (Lévis,
1903), p. 7; Benjamin Sulte, "Les 'Histoires' du Canada," *Revue
canadienne* 22 (1886): p. 457.

30. B. G. Reizov, *op. cit.,* pp. 241-243, 425.

31. Collingwood, *op. cit.,* p. 242.

32. *Ibid.*, p. 284.
33. W. H. Walsh, *op. cit.*, p. iii.
34. Herbert Butterfield, *George III and the Historians* (London, 1957); *The Whig Interpretation of History* (London, 1968); *Man on his past* (Cambridge, England, 1969).
35. Peter Geyl, *Debates with Historians* (The Hague, 1955).
36. Lewis P. Curtis, ed., *The Historian's Workshop* (New York, 1970).
37. Richard Hofstadter, *The Progressive Historians* (New York, 1970), p. 464.
38. Richard Hofstadter, *loc. cit.*
39. *American Historical Review* (AHR) vol. 52, no. 4 (July 1947), pp. 704-708.
40. Croce was unable to take up Beard's invitation, and instead wrote a letter of comments which was published together with "Written His-troy . . . ." AHR, vol. 39, no. 2 (January 1934), pp. 219-231.
41. *Ibid.*, p. 221. On Ranke, see also "That Noble Dream", AHR, vol. 40, no. 1 (1935), pp. 74-87.
42. R. A. Skotheim, *The Historian and the Climate of Opinion* (Reading, Mass., 1969), pp. 10, 11 and 210ff.
43. C. Wright Mills, *The Sociological Imagination* (New York, 1959).
44. C. Wright Mills, *The Marxists* (New York, 1962). See also the entry for Mills, in David L. Sills, ed., *The International Encyclopedia of the Social Sciences* (New York, 1968).
45. R. A. Skotheim, *op. cit.*, p. 136; S. M. Lipset, "Student Activists: a profile," *Dialogue* vol. 2, no. 2 (1969), pp. 6-7.
46. R. A. Skotheim, *op. cit.*, pp. 59-102.
47. *Ibid.*, pp. 103-163.
48. *Ibid.*, p. 118.
49. D. K. Rowney and J. Q. Graham, ed., *Quantitative History* (Georgetown, Ont., 1969).
50. John Higham, Leonard Krieger and Felix Gilbert, *History* (Englewood Cliffs, N.J., 1965); see especially pp. 6-25, 68-96.

Chapter II

1. W. J. McKeachie and C. L. Doyle, *Psychology* (London and Don Mills, Ont., 1966), pp. 323ff.
2. H. Piéron, *Vocabulaire de la psychologie* (Paris, 1968), under the word "témoignage." See also "La mémoire" in Denis Huisman, *Encyclopédie de la psychologie* (Paris, 1962), vol. 1, pp. 129-132.
3. Gordon W. Allport, in *The Use of Personal Documents in Psychological Sciences* (New York, 1941), p. xii; quoted by L. Gottschalk in "The Historian and the Historical Document" in Gottschalk et al., *The Use of Personal Documents in History, Anthropology and Sociology* (New York, 1945), pp. 1-75.
4. L. Gottschalk, *op. cit.*, p. 13 and note. Pp. 35 to 47. He presents the method known as internal criticism.
5. Marc Bloch, *The Historian's Craft* (New York, 1953). See pp. 79-137 on historical criticism.
6. Jean Hamelin, *Economie et société en Nouvelle-France* (Quebec, 1960), pp. 127f.

7. Pierre Vilar, "Histoire sociale et philosophie de l'histoire," *Recherches et Débats*, no. 47 (June 1964), pp. 56f.

8. "Serial history . . . is . . . 'less interested in the individual event . . . than in the repeated element . . . which can be integrated into a homogeneous series analysis. . . .'
   "The traffic which existed between Seville and the Americas from 1504 to 1650, reconstituted as to its original volume and value . . . 'a continuous body of quantified facts,'" as represented in Huguette and Pierre Chaunu's *Séville et L'Atlantique, 1550-1650* (Paris, S.E.V.P.E.N., 1959) is an example of serial history. See Fernand Braudel "Toward a Serial History: Seville and the Atlantic, 1504-1650" in his *On History* (Chicago, 1980), pp. 91-104.

9. Pierre Vilar, *op. cit.*

10. *Ibid.*, pp. 58f.

11. W. H. Walsh, *op. cit.*, p. 101.

12. Geoffrey Barraclough, *History in a Changing World* (London, 1955), p. 14; quoted by Carr, *op. cit.*, p. 14.

13. Jean Blain, "La frontière en Nouvelle-France," *Revue d'histoire de l'Amérique française* (RHAF), vol. 35, no. 3 (December 1971), p. 400.

14. L. Halphen, *Introduction à l'histoire* (Paris, 1948). See chapters 3 and 4, and in particular pp. 12, 16 and 26.

Chapter III

1. See Michel Brunet, "Trois dominantes de la pensée canadienne-française: l'agriculture, l'anti-étatisme et le messianisme," in *La Présence anglaise et les Canadiens* (Montreal, 1958), pp. 113-166; William F. Ryan, *The Clergy and Economic Growth in Quebec, 1896-1914* (Quebec, 1966); Joseph Levitt, "Henri Bourassa and Modern Industrial Society, 1900-1914." *Canadian Historical Review* (CHR), vol. 5, no. 1 (March 1969), pp. 37-50; and Joseph Levitt, *Henri Bourassa and the Golden Calf* (Ottawa, 1969).

2. Narcisse-Eutrope Dionne, *Vie de C.-F. Painchaud* (Quebec, 1894).

3. The author, Hélène Tassé, presented this work in a seminar on French-Canadian historiography in 1969.

4. See the *Dictionary of Canadian Biography*, vol. 2 (Toronto, 1969), pp. 439-445, under "Lom d'Arce de Lahontan, Louis-Armand de".

5. Joseph-Edmond Roy, *Le Baron de Lahontan, op. cit.*, p. 93.

6. Narcisse-Eutrope Dionne, "Inventaire des ouvrages publiés à l'étranger," *Mémoires de la Société royale du Canada*, section 1 (1905), p. 4.

7. Richard-Michel Bégin, "Etude comparée de L'Avenir et du Canada-Revue," M.A. thesis (Ottawa, 1972), p. 54.

8. *Joseph-Edmond Roy, op. cit.*, pp. 34 and 36-75.

9. *Ibid.*, p. 75; see also p. 76f.

10. *Ibid.*, p. 97.

11. *Ibid.*, pp. 77, 104.

12. *Ibid.*, p. 76.

13. *Ibid.*, pp. 117f.

14. *Ibid.*, p. 116.

15. *Ibid.*, pp. 163-196.
16. *Ibid.*, pp. 189-196.
17. See Gustave Lanctôt, *Faussaires et faussetés en histoire canadienne* (Montréal, 1948).
18. *Ibid.* Needless to say, the emergence of our institutes of history did not put an end to moralizing histories. Lanctôt's work is revealing in this respect. See in particular *Filles de joie ou filles du roi* (Montreal, 1952; 2nd edition 1964) and *Montréal sous Maisonneuve, 1642-1665* (Montreal, 1966).
19. Guy Frégault, *La Civilisation de la Nouvelle-France* (Montreal, 1944).

Chapter IV

1. *What is History?* p. 40.
2. *Ibid.*, p. 44.
3. *Ibid.*, p. 42.
4. Henri-Irénée Marrou, "La méthodologie historique: orientations actuelles." *Revue historique*, Vol. 209 (April-June 1953), p. 258. See also Marrou, *The Meaning of History, op. cit.*, pp. 287f.
5. Thus, for instance, in examining the evolution of French-Canadian historiography, one is struck by the fact that the generation of Guy Frégault (1918-1977), Marcel Trudel (1917-), Lucien Campeau (1914-) and Robert Lionel Séguin brought the study of New France to the forefront in the 1950s. The generation of Jean-Paul Bernard (1936-), Jean-Pierre Wallot (1935-) and Denis Vaugeois (1935-) has been concerned with the period from the Conquest to after 1837-38. A younger generation, composed of P.-A. Linteau (1946-), René Durocher, René Hardy, Fernand Harvey (1943-), Normand Séguin, Nadia Eid, etc., have concentrated almost exclusively on the period since 1850. On this shift in the periods constituting the focus of interest, see Fernand Harvey and Paul-André Linteau, "L'évolution de l'historiographie dans la RHAF, 1947-1972," RHAF vol. 26, no. 2, pp. 163-183.
6. Robert Escarpit, *Sociologie de la littérature*, Collection "Que sais-je?" (Paris, 1964). On production, see pp. 29-56; on consumption, pp. 99-125. See also John Hare, "Literature and Society," *Culture*, vol. 26, no. 4 (December 1965), pp. 412-423.
7. Paul Ricoeur, *History and Truth*, translated by Charles A. Kelbley (Evanston, 1965), p. 32.

Chapter V

1. John Hexter sees historiography as "a branch of intellectual history or a subbranch of the sociology of knowledge." Cf. David L. Sills, ed. *International Encyclopedia of the Social Sciences, op. cit.*, vol. 6, p. 368 under "Historiography." In England, the discipline has also been practised as a form of the sociology of knowledge; see G. R. Elton, *Modern Historians, op. cit.*, p. 188.
2. Georges Gurvitch, *The Social Frameworks of Knowledge*, translated

by Margaret A. Thompson and Kenneth A. Thompson (Oxford, 1971), p. 12.

3. *Ibid.*, p. 10.

4. *Ibid.*, p. 17. See also one of his last articles on the subject: "La Sociologie de la connaissance," *Revue de l'Enseignement supérieur*, no. 1-2 (Jan.-June 1965), pp. 43-51. Lewis A. Coser attributes the same goals to the discipline in "Sociology of Knowledge," *International Encyclopedia of the Social Sciences*, *op. cit.*, vol. 8, p. 428. See also Pierre Delooz, *Sociologie et canonisation* (Liège, La Haye, 1969). In addition to summing up the state of the art in the sociology of knowledge, this book is an excellent empirical test of the discipline.

5. R. A. Skotheim, *American Intellectual Histories and Historians* (Princeton, 1966), pp. 299ff.

6. Robin W. Winks, ed., *The Historiography of the British Empire-Commonwealth* (Durham, N.C., 1966). His article on Canada is to be found pp. 69-136, and the quotation on p. 72.

7. Joseph-Edmond Roy, *Histoire de la seigneurie de Lauzon*, 5 vols. (Lévis, 1897-1904); Thomas Chapais, *Jean Talon, intendant de la Nouvelle-France, 1665-1672* (Quebec, 1904), and *Le Marquis de Montcalm, 1712-1759* (Quebec, 1911).

8. Séraphin Marion, *Relations des voyageurs français en Nouvelle-France au XVIIe siècle* (Paris, 1923); Paul-Emile Renaud, *Les Origines économiques du Canada* (Mamers, 1928); Gustave Lanctôt, *L'Administration de la Nouvelle-France* (Paris, 1929); and Antoine Roy, *Les Lettres, les sciences et les arts au Canada sous le régime français* (Paris, 1930).

9. These comments are based on our systematic analysis of the histories written of New France between 1845 and 1915.

10. Winks, *op. cit.*, p. 70.

11. Lionel Groulx, "Un Seigneur en soutane," RHAF, vol. 11 no. 2 (September 1957), pp. 204f., note 3.

12. Paul Wyczynski, "Panorama du roman canadien-français," in Archives des lettres canadiennes, vol. 3, *Le Roman canadien-français* (Montreal, 1964), p. 19.

13. N.-E. Dionne, *Jacques Cartier* (Quebec, 1889); Marcel Trudel, *Histoire de la Nouvelle-France, Vol. 1, Les vaines tentatives 1524-1603* (Montreal, 1963), pp. 65-175, and in particular pp. 70, 81f., 88, 99 and 123.

Chapter VI

1. Maurice Halbwachs, *la Mémoire collective,* Coll. "Bibliotèque de sociologie contemporaine" (Paris, 1968); published in English as *The Collective Memory*, translated by Francis J. Ditter Jr. and Vida Yazdi Ditter (New York, 1980).

2. *Ibid.*, pp. 50-56, "Le Lien vivant des générations."

3. *Ibid.*, pp. 68-79.

4. Marc Bloch, *Feudal Society*, translated by L. A. Manyon (Chicago, 1964), ch. 6, pp. 88-102; Halbwachs, *op. cit.*, p. 50, refers to "La mémoire collective, traditions et coutumes," published by Marc Bloch in 1925 in the *Revue de synthèse historique*.

5. Jean Stoetzel, *La Psychologie sociale* (Paris, 1963). See chapter 8, "La mémoire," pp. 111-122.
6. Lucien Goldman comments on Weber's observation in *Sciences humaines et philosophie. Qu'est-ce que la sociologie* (Paris, 1966), p. 27. See also Raymond Aron, *Introduction to the Philosophy of History, op. cit.;* and Alfred Stern, *La Philosophie de l'histoire et le problème des valeurs* (Paris, 1959), pp. 99-110. On the same question, see Collingwood, *op. cit.,* pp. 235ff.
7. Pierre Janet, *L'Evolution de la mémoire et de la notion du temps,* 3 vols. (Paris, 1928); quoted by Jean Guillaumin in *La Genèse du souvenir* (Paris, 1968), p. 182.
8. Guy Rocher, *A General Introduction to Sociology: a Theoretical Perspective,* translated by Peta Sheriff (Toronto, 1972), p. 78.
9. Jean Naud, *Structure et sens du symbole : L'imaginaire chez Gaston Bachelard* (Montreal, 1971). See the chapter on "Imagination et mémoire," pp. 23-61, and in particular pp. 24f.
10. *Ibid.,* pp. 58f., note 39.
11. Denis Huisman, *op. cit.,* vol. 1, p. 132.
12. Raymond Aron, *Introduction to the Philosophy of History, op. cit.,* p. 319.
13. J. Momsen, "The Development of Scholarly Historical Study," *op. cit.,* p. 123.
14. Carr, *op. cit.,* p. 25.
15. Sulte to Malchelosse, April 9, 1914, Archives of the Université Laval, Quebec. Unclassified collection.
16. R. S. Lynd, *Knowledge for What?* (Princeton, 1939), p. 88; quoted in Carr, *op. cit.,* p. 116, note 1.
17. B. G. Reizov, *op. cit.*
18. On the origins of the idea of the Conquest as providential, see Claude Galarneau, *La France devant l'opinion canadienne, 1760-1815* (Quebec, 1970), pp. 336-339. This was the dominant theme in historical writing for nearly a century. It has been rejected by neo-nationalists. See André Beaulieu, Jean Hamelin and Benoit Bernier, *Guide d'histoire du Canada* (Quebec, 1969), pp. 42-45. Neo-nationalism was pessimistic during the 1950s but later became optimistic, giving rise to the idea of Quebec's independence. The sociology of colonialism and decolonization are especially helpful in understanding the significance of the neo-nationalist theses. On this, see Guy Rocher, *op. cit.,* pp. 497-525.

Chapter VII

1. Henri-Irénée Marrou, *The Meaning of History, op. cit.,* p. 302.
2. Fernand Dumont, "Structure d'une idéologie religieuse," *Recherches sociographiques,* no. 2 (April-June 1960): pp. 168f.
3. Rocher, *op. cit.,* p. 103.
4. Fernand Dumont, "Idéologie et savoir historique," *Cahiers internationaux de sociologie,* vol. 35 (July-December 1963), p. 54.
5. *Ibid.,* p. 60.

Chapter VIII

1. Laurent Giroux, *Durée et temporalité: Bergson et Heidegger* (Montreal, 1971).
2. Paul Veyne, "Statut scientifique de l'histoire," *op. cit.*, p. 60.
3. Raymond Aron, *Dimensions de la conscience historique* (Paris, 1971), Coll. "Le monde en 10/18," p. 39.
4. Raymond Aron, *Introduction to the Philosophy of History, op. cit.*, p. 312.
5. *Ibid.*, p. 334.
6. *Ibid.*, p. 279.
7. *Ibid.*, p. 335.
8. *Ibid.*, p. 100.
9. Raymond Aron, *Dimensions, op. cit.*, p. 16.
10. H.-I. Marrou, *The Meaning of History, op. cit.*, pp. 214-215.
11. G. R. Elton, *The Practice of History* (New York, 1967), pp. 39f.
12. Benedetto Croce, *History as the Story of Liberty, op. cit.*, pp. 17-18. On what Carr owes to Croce, see Carr, *op. cit.*, pp. 20-21.
13. Croce, *ibid.*, p. 24.
14. *Ibid.*, p. 59.
15. Quoted by J. R. Hale, *The Evolution of British Historiography* (Cleveland and New York, 1964), pp. 41f.
16. Quoted by H. Butterfield, *Man on his Past, op. cit.*, pp. 11f.
17. *Ibid.*, p. 12, note 1.
18. Gabriel Hanotaux, *De l'histoire et des historiens* (Paris, 1919), p. 13.
19. Fernand Ouellet, *Economic and Social History of Quebec, 1760-1850* (Ottawa, 1980), p. xvii.
20. *Ibid.*, p. xxii.
21. Carr, *op. cit.*, p. 123.
22. Boyd C. Shafer, *op. cit.*, p. 27.
23. Richard Hofstadter, *op. cit.*, p. 465.
24. H.-I. Marrou, *The Meaning of History, op. cit.*, p. 216.
25. Carl L. Becker, *Everyman His Own Historian* (New York, 1935), p. 253.
26. Quoted by John Higham, *op. cit.*, p. 127.
27. Georges Lefebvre, *Notions d'historiographie moderne* (Paris, 1946), re-edited as *La Naissance de l'historiographie moderne* (Paris, 1971), p. 16; Halkin, *op. cit.*, p. 24; Walsh, *op. cit.*, pp. 109 and 185-187; Butterfield, *op. cit.*, p. 25; and Carr, *op. cit.*, p. 69.

Chapter IX

1. Fernand Dumont, "Idéologie et savoir historique," *op. cit.*, p. 60.
2. Elton criticized Carr for describing history as "highly selective." See *The Practice of History, op. cit.*, pp. 39-50.
3. Chaïm Pérelman, "Objectivité et intelligibilité dans la connaissance historique" in Pérelman, ed., *Raisonnement et démarches de l'historien* (Brussels, 1963), pp. 146f.
4. Raymond Aron, *Introduction to the Philosophy of History, op. cit.*, p. 299, in the conclusion to his comments on Durkheim and Simiand.

5. Charles Beard, "Written history" (AHR, Vol. 39), p. 222; also see "That Noble Dream," *op. cit.*, p. 77.
6. W. H. Walsh, *op. cit.*, pp. 97f; Dray, *Philosophy of History* (Prentice-Hall, N.J., 1964), pp. 27f; Beard, "That Noble Dream," *op. cit.*, pp. 83f; and Stern, *op. cit.*, pp. 99-110.
7. Georges Lefebvre, *La Naissance de l'historiographie moderne, op. cit.*, p. 17.
8. *Ibid.*, p. 18.
9. *Ibid.*, p. 19.
10. Gottschalk et al., *The Use of Personal Documents, op. cit.*, p. 50.
11. *Ibid.*, p. 51.
12. Carr, *op. cit.*, p. 12.
13. Cf. H.-I. Marrou, *The Meaning of History, op. cit.*, p. 31; Raymond Aron, *Introduction to the Philosophy of History, op. cit.*, p. 97; Robert Jones Shafer, *A Guide to Historical Method* (Homewood, Ill., and Georgetown, Ont., 1969), p. 15.
14. Cameron Nish, "Hagiographie canadienne contemporaine," *Revue du centre d'étude du Québec*, no. 3 (May 1969), pp. 20-23.
15. Marcel Trudel, *Chiniquy* (Trois-Rivières, 1955).
16. W. J. C. Cherwinski, "The Left in Canadian History, 1911-1969," *Journal of Canadian Studies* (November 1969), pp. 51-60.
17. Alfred Dubuc, "Le Rapport Parent et l'enseignement de l'histoire," *Socialisme*, no. 5 (Spring 1965), pp. 109-118.

Chapter X

1. W. H. Walsh, *op. cit.*, pp. 99-103.
2. Jean Provencher, *Québec sous la loi des mesures de guerre 1918* (Montreal, 1971).
3. *Ibid.*, p. 8
4. Jean-Claude Leclerc, in an editorial in *Le Devoir*, February 1, 1972.
5. W. H. Walsh, *op. cit.*, p. 112, note 1.
6. Boyd C. Shafer, *op. cit.*, p. 24.
7. André Beaulieu, Jean Hamelin and Benoit Bernier, *Guide d'histoire du Canada* (Quebec, 1969), pp. 456ff.
8. It has begun to give rise to works on specialized methods; see, for example, André Nouschi, *Initiation aux sciences historiques* (Paris, 1967).
9. We distinguish the causal interpretation from the narrative interpretation. On this, see John Hexter, *op. cit.* On causality, see also Morton White, *Foundations of Historical Knowledge* (New York and London, 1965), pp. 105-181 (the chapter "Causal Interpretation").
10. Fernand Ouellet, *Histoire économique et sociale,* op. cit.
11. For the neo-nationalist interpretation, see in particular Maurice Séguin, *La Nation "canadienne" et l'agriculture* (Montreal, 1970).
12. Jan Crayebeck, "La notion d'importance à la lumière de l'histoire moderne" in Chaïm Pérelman, *Raisonnement et démarches, op. cit.*, p. 67.

Chapter XI

1. On Simiand, see Aron, *Introduction to the Philosophy of History, op. cit.*, pp. 185-186 and 213-224; on Durkheim and Weber, see pp. 201-207 and 266-271; on the limits of statistical causality, pp. 208ff; see also pp. 156-263 passim.
2. F.-A. Isambert, *Buchez ou l'âge théologique de la sociologie: Politique, religion et science de l'homme chez Philippe Buchez, 1796-1865* (Paris, 1968). On the history of sociological theory, see Raymond Aron, *Les Étapes de la pensée sociologique* (Paris, 1967).
3. It is noteworthy that *Introduction aux études historiques* (1895) was published almost simultaneously with *The Rules of Sociological Method* (first published in French in 1898).
4. Alfred Dubuc, "Le Rapport Parent" *op. cit.*
5. Alfred Dubuc, "L'Histoire au carrefour des sciences humaines," RHAF, vol. 24, no. 3 (December 1970), p. 340.
6. Fernand Dumont, "Du Sociologisme à la crise des fondements en sociologie," *Recherches et Débats*, no. 25, p. 92.
7. Fernand Dumont, "Note sur l'analyse des idéologies," *Recherches sociographiques*, vol. 4, no. 2 (May-August 1963), p. 155.
8. Fernand Dumont, "L'Étude systématique de la société globale canadienne-française," *Recherches sociographiques*, vol. 3, no. 1-2 (January-August 1962), pp. 278f, and note 1 for the second quotation.
9. In historiography, see reviews by Québécois of Mason Wade's *The French Canadians, 1760-1945*, for instance, Guy Frégault in the RHAF, vol. 8, no. 4 (March 1955), pp. 582-583. Maurice Héroux also reviewed the book in *Culture*, 16 (1955), pp. 352-354, in the context of neo-nationalism. In *Relations*, no. 172 (April 1955), Richard Arès reviewed it in the light of traditional eccesiastical nationalism. In sociography, see the house critique of the Chicago school of sociology by Philippe Garigue, *Etudes sur le Canada français* (Montreal, 1958), pp. 5-16.
10. Chaïm Pérelman and L. Olbrechts-Typeca, *La Nouvelle rhétorique: traité de l'argumentation* (Paris, 1958), 1: 22-53.
11. Chaïm Pérelman, *Raisonnement et démarches, op. cit.*, pp. 144f.

Index